# The Secret War Against Red Russia

The Daring Exploits of Paul Dukes
and Augustus Agar VC
During the Russian Civil War

Brian Best

FRONTLINE BOOKS

First published in Great Britain in 2022 by
Frontline Books
An imprint of
Pen & Sword Books Ltd
Yorkshire – Philadelphia

ISBN 978 1 39909 065 0

Typeset by Mac Style
Printed in the UK by CPI Group (UK) Ltd, Croydon, CR0 4YY.

Pen & Sword Books Limited incorporates the imprints of Atlas,
Archaeology, Aviation, Discovery, Family History, Fiction, History,
Maritime, Military, Military Classics, Politics, Select, Transport,
True Crime, Air World, Frontline Publishing, Leo Cooper, Remember
When, Seaforth Publishing, The Praetorian Press, Wharncliffe
Local History, Wharncliffe Transport, Wharncliffe True Crime
and White Owl.

For a complete list of Pen & Sword titles please contact

PEN & SWORD BOOKS LIMITED
47 Church Street, Barnsley, South Yorkshire, S70 2AS, England
E-mail: enquiries@pen-and-sword.co.uk
Website: www.pen-and-sword.co.uk

Or

PEN AND SWORD BOOKS
1950 Lawrence Rd, Havertown, PA 19083, USA
E-mail: Uspen-and-sword@casematepublishers.com
Website: www.penandswordbooks.com

# Contents

| | | |
|---|---|---|
| *Introduction* | | vi |
| Chapter 1 | The One-Legged Chief | 1 |
| Chapter 2 | The Death of Captain Francis Cromie | 6 |
| Chapter 3 | The Agents | 16 |
| Chapter 4 | The Newspaper Reporters | 28 |
| Chapter 5 | Enter Paul Dukes | 39 |
| Chapter 6 | Lieutenant Augustus Agar | 58 |
| Chapter 7 | Dukes' Second Visit | 67 |
| Chapter 8 | Agar Searches For a Base | 75 |
| Chapter 9 | The Sinking of the *Oleg* | 86 |
| Chapter 10 | Walter Cowan | 97 |
| Chapter 11 | March 1919 | 103 |
| Chapter 12 | Dobson's Kronstadt Raid | 109 |
| Chapter 13 | Kronstadt Raid | 115 |
| Chapter 14 | Agar's Return to the Baltic | 134 |
| Chapter 15 | Dukes' Departure from Petrograd | 141 |
| Chapter 16 | Agar's Return to the Baltic | 148 |
| Chapter 17 | Paul Dukes as a Private Eye | 157 |
| Chapter 18 | Agar's Final Years | 160 |
| *Bibliography* | | 170 |

# Introduction

The Armistice of 11 November 1918 ended four years of slaughter that had left the participants exhausted and the populations weary of war. One such mess that had been left was the unresolved problem of Russia and its Revolution that was threatening to engulf the Baltic States and Poland. The Russian Civil War of 1918–22 arose from the cataclysmic events of the First World War and dwarfed all others in scope and significance. There was little sympathy for the Tsarist regime and much suspicion for the Bolsheviks (a slang word for 'more men'), which left the British caught between a rock and a hard place. Without a clear and firm policy, the Intelligence Service was given free rein to obtain information on what was happening in Russia. The public had little interest in the Russian Revolution, and Britain's brief military involvement in Russia lasted some six months. In September 1918, the British decided to send a force to the northern ports of Murmansk and Archangel to reclaim the supplies they had sent during the war. In doing so, Britain became involved in a short, fruitless and largely forgotten conflict, which, nonetheless, produced five Victoria Cross actions.

The Secret Service came into force during the Edwardian period, when Britain and Germany were building warships which were progressively improving. In 1909 a joint initiative of the Admiralty and the War Office saw the start of two separate secret sections; the MI5 and MI6. The first director of MI6 (SIS) was Captain Sir George Mansfield Smith-Cumming, who typically signed his correspondence with a 'C' in green ink, had a wooden leg and a craze for speed. His opposite director was Vernon Kel, a former head of the German Section of the War Office who was installed as head of MI5. The need for a well-financed secret service was impressed on Viscount Haldane, the Secretary of State for War. Most intelligence officers came from the middle class – being the sons of military men – and this gradually became less of a burden to the Secret Service as the decades followed.

On 28 December 1918, Cumming called on Lord Hardinge at the Foreign Office and secured his permission 'to our continuing our organisation in Russia at £3,000 a month until 31 March.' Intervention in Russia began as an effort to shore up Russian forces fighting against the Central Powers, but after the Soviet government signed a peace treaty in the spring of 1918 with Germany, Britain and its allies found themselves aligned with counter-revolutionary White Russian elements in an escalating Russian civil war. The SIS activities in Russia had purely information gathering purposes but they became involved with direct anti-Soviet operations.

One of the major assassinations that took place during the First World War was that of Gregori Rasputin. During the lead-up to the Russian Revolution, he was a divisive figure coming from peasant stock, but was seen as a mystic and a prophet. In 1906 he acted as healer to the tsar's only son, Alexei, who suffered from haemophilia, and was regarded by the royal couple as a visionary. The royal couple's physician, Doctor Fedorov, admitted that the tsarina could not be blamed for thinking Rasputin was a miracle man. 'Rasputin would come in, walk up to the patient, look at him, and spit. The bleeding would stop in no time ... How could the Empress not trust Rasputin after that?'

Rasputin had a darker side and was a drunken debaucher. He seemed to have a hold over the tsar's family and there were many of the court who wished him dead. He held a mystic sway over the Royal Family and was influential in late Imperial Russia. One attempt on his life occurred on 12 July 1914 when a peasant woman named Chionya Guseva attempted to stab Rasputin in the stomach outside his home in Pokrovskoye. He was seriously wounded and thought he would die, but after surgery he rallied and made a good recovery.

His final demise occurred on 30 December 1916, when a group of nobles led by Prince Felix Yusupov lured him to Moika Palace in Petrograd (St Petersburg's name between 1914–24) with a view to killing him. The exact events surrounding Rasputin's death are still vague and in dispute. Felix Yusupov was the ring leader and he invited Rasputin to a small but lavishly decorated cellar room in the Moika Palace. He was served red wine until he became drunk. Yusupov obtained a revolver and shot Rasputin in the side leaving him for dead. Rushing upstairs, Yusupov told the other conspirators that he had killed Rasputin. Driving to Rasputin's apartment in an attempt to look as if he had returned home, they pretended to drop off Rasputin and return to Moika Palace. Rasputin found a gated doorway to a courtyard, stumbled and was shot in the back by Vladimir Purishkevich, one of the accomplices. Taking the body inside, Rasputin was killed by a third bullet fired at close range which entered his forehead. The conspirators tied his hands together and wrapped the body in broadcloth, drove to the outskirts of the city and threw the body into the Little Nevka River. It would seem probable that Oswald Raynor – a British agent and friend – was involved, as he had a Webley revolver with him and is said to have fired the fatal shot into Rasputin's head. As with most agents, he managed to fade into the background. He was supported by John Scale, bureau chief in Stockholm, and Stephen Alley, who wrote to Scale:

> Although matters have not proceeded entirely to plan, our objective has clearly been achieved. Reaction to the demise of Dark Forces (a codename for Rasputin) has been well received by all, although a few awkward questions have already been asked about wider involvement. Raynor is attending to loose ends and will no doubt brief you on your return.

In 1916 Scale served with Stephen Alley and Oswald Raynor under Mansfield Cumming at the time of Rasputin's murder. Several books and documents recorded Scale's involvement in Rasputin's death, including his order to Raynor to shoot the priest. As a side issue, Rasputin's daughter, Maria, left Russia when the October Revolutions broke out and worked as a dancer in France before becoming a lion tamer in America.

Proving no match for the German and Austro-Hungarian forces on the Eastern Front, the Russian army, although huge in size, quickly collapsed. Only the Czechoslovak Legion of 50,000 fought with the Central Powers – albeit reluctantly – and when the Russian army divided between the Whites and the Bolsheviks, it remained an effective fighting force. The cessation of hostilities did not bring peace to Europe but stirred up struggles for social change and national identity. The conflict for Russia between the Bolsheviks and the White Russians had encouraged the Baltic States of Estonia, Latvia, Lithuania, Poland and Finland – all former imperial provinces – to declare their independence. Prime Minister Lloyd George's government was undecided as to how to react to events in Russia. Germany was still perceived as the main enemy and it therefore backed the side that would keep Russia fighting on the Eastern Front. There seemed to be little sympathy or support for the deposed Tsarist regime but the anti-Bolshevik White Russians seemed the lesser of the two evils and were given half-hearted support by the British government. As the increasingly bitter civil war grew in ferocity, the Bolsheviks showed more determination and began to show their true colours. Despite the war, Great Britain was regarded as the main stumbling block, and in Russia foreigners were regarded with great suspicion and were frequently attacked.

Vladimir Ilyich Ulyanov – better known by his alias, Lenin – was in exile for ten years in Switzerland and had negotiated a passage through Germany to Petrograd. The Germans realised that the far-left leader would stir up much trouble in Russia and even call a cessation to Russia's involvement in the war. The Germans chartered a 'sealed' train provided by Kaiser Wilhelm II with the aim of furthering the Bolshevik Revolution. On 9 April 1917, thirty-two Russian émigrés waited at Zurich railway station to depart, singing *'The Internationale'* and were sent on their way with a demonstration of shouts of 'traitors and scoundrels'. The tracks were blocked for a short while, but soon the train was trundling its way north to the port of Sassnitz. From there they boarded a ferry to take them to Sweden, where they caught a train to Petrograd. Lenin and his followers arrived at the Finland Station, where he made a speech from an armoured car to his Bolshevik comrades, condemning the Provisional Government and calling for a Europe-wide proletarian revolution. Among the crowd who witnessed Lenin's arrival were three Englishmen; Paul Dukes, Arthur Ransome and William Gibson. Germany's top generals sent a message to the Federal Foreign Office saying, 'Lenin's entry into Russia was a success. He is working according to your wishes.'

One of the major fibs that the Bolsheviks used was the October Revolution. Before that, leaders of the Bolsheviks were scattered around the world and the March Revolution of 1917 which was far more radical and has almost been forgotten. Lenin was still in Zurich, Trotsky was in America and Stalin was about to be released from Siberia. In Petrograd many thousands of women marched in protest at the bread shortages to be joined by 170,000 troops. This early revolution saw the downfall of the tsar, the installation of the Socialist Provisional Government led by Alexander Kerensky, and unfortunately the continuation of the disintegration of the Eastern Front. Coincidentally, both Lenin and Kerensky – leaders of their respective parties – came from the same town, Simbirsk on the Volga River. They both had Jewish blood and both had studied law at university. Another interesting fact was that the young Lenin had briefly been taught by Kerensky's father.

In July the Bolsheviks attempted to overthrow the Provisional Government in a failed coup. Kerensky arranged for General Krymov's 3rd Cavalry Corps to enter Petrograd, root out disloyal elements and save Russia. Ordering that the arsenals to be opened to arm Petrograd's left-wing, he called upon all partisans to take up key points to control the city. Unfortunately, the Bolsheviks quickly rallied and took control and by October they began their own revolution, a poor relation to the March one.

The Russian Civil War started at the end of the most disastrous four years of the First World War. Few of the Allies, which included Germany and the Austrian-Hungarian Dual Alliance, showed any inclination to become involved in a war that spread across the world's largest country. The Germans realised that the dissidents would cause problems amongst the Allies, and Berlin's strategy was for Lenin and his followers to destabilize Russia in the middle of the First World War and ease the burden of fighting on the Eastern Front.

Winston Churchill, writing in his six-volume, *The World Crisis*, gave his view of the First World War. He claimed that Germany gave permission to Lenin to travel through their country, which changed Russia for over seventy years. He wrote of Lenin's return, 'It was with a sense of awe that they turned upon Russia the most grisly of all weapons. They transported Lenin in a sealed truck like a plague bacillus into Russia.'

With the help of Germany, weapons and dynamite crossed the Sweden-Finland border. Aided by Israel Lazarevich Gelfand, a communist but also a classic war profiteer whose 'gifts' helped to sink ships at Archangel and other ports. His actions were coordinated with the German ambassador in Copenhagen, who believed 'supporting the communists was justified if it helped destroy the war coalition.' Gelfand's plan bore fruit, for on 7 November 1917 the Soviets seized power in the October Revolution. Although the kaiser had spent around 2 million marks, Lenin was accused of accepting German money. To this charge, he countered with;

'I would, however, like to add that we will stage a similar revolution in Germany with Russian money.'

Lenin assumed leadership of the Bolshevik (majority) movement. His deputy, Leon Trotsky, became a member of the Menshevik (minority) party and developed his theory of 'permanent revolution'. Despite disagreements with Lenin, he left the Mensheviks and joined the Bolsheviks, playing a decisive role in the communist takeover of power in 1917–18. He took part in the Brest-Litovsk peace talks, was made war commissar and built up the Red Army that eventually beat the White Russian forces. He saw himself as taking over from Lenin, who died in January 1924 after having several strokes, but his arrogance made him few friends. Trotsky refused to attend Lenin's funeral, having revolted against the New Economic Policy and within a year was ousted from the Communist Party. Josef Stalin became the overall leader and Trotsky was forced into exile. In 1940 he was killed in his home in Mexico with an ice axe wielded by Ramon Mercader, a Soviet NKVD agent.

In February 1917 food riots broke out in Petrograd and other major Russian cities, and police dressed as soldiers were sent to stamp out the disorder. Ordered by the tsar, the soldiers were told to fire into the crowd, but they refused. They instead sided with the protestors as law and order broke down, and a new liberal government took over the running of the country. The Duma (Parliament) was situated in the Tauride Palace but was unable to govern the country as it was made up of different factions and ideas. Petrograd was especially devastated because it was not near any agriculturally-rich areas and only received a third of its fuel and goods despite its massive population. The workers in the huge Putilov Mill went on strike in the winter and sparked the March Revolution, declaring that:

On 10 March a mass meeting was held at the Putilov Works. 10,000 men were present and the following resolutions were passed with only twenty-two dissentients, all of whom were strangers unconnected with the Works ... the labouring classes of Russia and the world that the Bolshevist Government had betrayed the ideals of the revolution, and thus betrayed and deceived the workers and peasants in Russia; that the Bolshevist Government, acting in our names, is not the authority of the proletariat and peasants, but a dictatorship of the Bolshevik party. We protest against the compulsion of workmen to remain tied to factories and works, and the attempt to deprive them of elementary rights, freedom of speech, press, meetings, inviolability of person, etc. We demand the release of workers and their wives who have been arrested; the restoration of a free press, free speech, right of meeting, inviolability of person; transfer of food administration to co-operative societies; and transfer of power to freely elected worker's and peasant's soviets.

These grand words were followed by another war with Poland, famine and dictatorship. Paul Dukes wrote in his book, *The Story of ST 25*, about the strength to the Cheka.

I doubt very much whether the workers, even had their leaders not been arrested, were sufficiently armed and organised to have overcome the Cheka forces, but the prime reason for their failure, as for the failure of every other similar rising against the Bolsheviks, was that from its inception the Cheka had planted spies and informers in the factories to show up the worker's ringleaders. The latter were seized with their wives and families deported to distant regions and never heard of again.

Continuing mounting criticism and violent reaction to his policies, the tsar decided to abdicate in favour of his younger brother, Grand Duke Michael. This did not work as he did not have the support of the peasants, the police and the armed forces. The rest of Europe thought Russia was entering a new democratic era by replacing the autocratic rule of the tsars. During this short period of democracy, freedom of speech, religious worship and an end to censorship of the press rose briefly before being suppressed by the Bolsheviks.

The revolution broke out during March 1917. William Gibson, a Canadian who had married the daughter of an aristocratic lady, had been watching as the street mob ransacked the mansions and palaces, and would soon reach his mother-in-law's marbled residence. Madame Schwartz-Ebehard, a pillar of the old order, was described by Gibson as 'a massive woman of forty-five, with tight lips and eyes which could turn to steel ... a veritable tower of strength, both physically and morally.' Gibson made his way to warn his mother-in-law that the mob would barge their way into her house and wreak much damage. As he reached the residence, Madame had confronted the mob.

> Seizing the gong-stick from the brass Chinese gong which filled the corner, she pointed at the highly polished marble floor and then glared at the thugs. The men stopped in their tracks. Madame had drawn herself to full height and stared the rabble down. 'Your boots are filthy. You should have cleaned them before you came in here. You are spoiling the floor – besides, you are not invited.'
>
> Informing them that they were 'scum of the gutters', she ordered them out. She had no intention of being intimidated by revolutionaries. The men lifted their rifles and pointed them at her, but Madame swept them aside. Calmly and deliberately she smacked the face of one desperado after another. Then, after forcing the ringleader backwards, she kicked them out and locked the door. She was fortunate to escape with her life. In her glacial haughtiness, she personified the social grandeur of the old regime. Now these days were in danger of being trampled underfoot.

After the short-lived Provisional Duma, the Bolsheviks changed the lives of millions through death, disease, imprisonment, execution and famine. Russia was plunged into the bloodiest civil war of the century and the most explosive political development of the twentienth century. Why were the Bolsheviks so successful in their October Revolution? They were aided by the weakness of the Provisional Government headed by Kerensky, who wished to carry on the war against Germany. This did not appeal to the thousands of peasant soldiers who had been sent to the front. He could not see that the costly and devastating defeats contributed to the economic problems that afflicted the Russian people. Kerensky was keen to dispense with the tsarist system which kept the royalists on top with the ignorant peasants toiling away at the bottom. He was anxious to modernise the country and adopt a democratic system which would allow the population to vote for a government every four or so years. Unable to hear what the Russian people had to say about the war, he went ahead and continued the conflict against Germany.

By October 1917 another revolution had broken out and the Kerensky Government had been ousted by the Bolsheviks. The new regime wanted complete control without the distraction of fighting the Germans and began to negotiate a separate peace. The Bolsheviks were the only party who opposed the capitalist war, which appealed to a large section of the population. The Russian army began to crumble, with the army officers refusing to fight for the Provisional Government and ignoring the growing strength of the Bolsheviks. As the popularity of the Bolsheviks increased, they took over from Kerensky's government and imposed a rigid oppression.

The October Revolution began in an effort to remove Alexander Kerensky, the leader of the Socialist Revolutionary Party. He had been voted in to guide the Russian people to a more moderate state, but by 7 November 1917 his government had been overthrown by the Lenin-Bolsheviks. Although Kerensky's cabinet were hiding in the Winter Palace, he managed to escape – not in a woman's dress as the Soviets alleged, but in an American embassy car. He went into exile in Paris, Prague and the United States. He died in 1970, aged 89, in New York but the Russian Orthodox Church refused a burial because of Kerensky's association with Freemasonry. He was also refused a burial because the Bolsheviks had seized power fifty years prior and he was powerless to prevent them from taking over and running the country. Instead, his body was flown to London and he was buried in Putney Vale cemetery later in 1970.

John Reed, a communist who wrote the classic book *Ten Days That Shook the World*, wrote about the Bolshevik Revolution. In spite of the looting of prescious items, he wrote the following words. Despite the pilfering Reed managed to hide a jewelled sword in his clothes.

A number of huge packing cases stood about, and upon these the Red Guards and soldiers fell furiously, battering them open with the butts of their rifles, and pulling out carpets, curtains, linen, porcelain plates, glass-ware … One man went strutting around with a bronze clock perched on his shoulder; another found a plume of ostrich feathers, which he stuck in his hat. The looting was just beginning when someone cried, 'Comrades! Don't take anything. This is the property of the People!' Immediately twenty voices were crying, 'Stop! Put everything back! Don't take anything! Property of the People!' Many hands pulled the spoilers down. Damask and tapestry were snatched from the arms of those who had them; two men took away the bronze clock. Roughly and hastily the things were crammed back in their cases, and self-appointed sentinels stood guard. It was all utterly spontaneous…

It was now after three in the morning. On the Nevsky all the street-lights were again shining, the cannon gone, and the only signs of war were the Red Guards and soldiers squatting around fires. The city was quiet – probably never so quiet in its history; on that night not a single hold-up occurred, not a single robbery.

In early March 1917 the Kerensky Government placed Tsar Nicholas, his wife and family in the Alexander Palace at Tsarskove Selo, about 24 miles south of Petrograd. They were soon moved again to protect them from the increasing revolutionary fervour and placed them in Tobolsk in the Ural Mountains. When the Bolsheviks overcame the Provisional Government in October, Kerensky lost control of the tsar's family. The conditions of the tsar's family grew stricter as the White movement grew stronger. In May 1918 the Bolsheviks transferred the family to Yekaterinburg, a Bolshevik stronghold, and on 16 July – whether ordered by Lenin or the Bolsheviks officials – the family were taken to the cellar and executed.

Mansfield Cumming's Russian Bureau was housed in the Petrograd War Ministry before the second revolution of 1917. The agents continued to send intelligence reports back to Whitehall Court, although it was difficult to get a clear picture of what was happening during these chaotic times. On 7 November 1917 British ambassador Sir George Buchanan noticed that armoured cars had taken up positions around the Winter Palace. The fierce battle that took place in Sergei Eisenstein's 1927 film *October* did not happen. The garrison of 2,000 soldiers had dwindled until all that was left were three squadrons of Cossacks, a handful of volunteers and a company from the Women's Battalion of Death. Buchanan was further surprised when the cruiser *Aurora* fired a blank shot, which was a signal for the mob of Bolsheviks to move on the palace. They met very little resistance and the famous battle for the Winter Palace was pure propaganda.

Lenin later delivered his proclamation calling for the transfer of all privately-owned land into the hands of the local councils. He also called for an immediate end of Russia's participation in the war against Germany and a dramatic call for revolution in the Western democracies. Later

Trotsky made a speech at the giant Putilov engineering works where he promised the Bolsheviks would improve the conditions of the workmen. Instead, he was planning to requisition two large churches for the workers. At this point a worker rose and interrupted, saying; 'Tovarishch Trotsky, instead of taking our churches, which are badly heated and unsuited to your requirements, why do you not requisition your synagogue in Offizerskaya Street, which would suit you better?' This interruption was followed by deadly silence. Trotsky made no reply and the interrupter followed with; 'I was sure I should be seized and arrested, and I was in mortal fear, but to my astonishment, I am still at liberty.'

At the end of the First World War, the Chief of the Imperial General Staff, Sir Henry Wilson, declared that the real danger now was not the Boche but Bolshevism. Russian communism dominated British domestic and foreign policy through to the end of the twentieth century. After the Second World War the Soviet Union planted agents in African and Central American countries in an effort to undermine Western democracies, but in the late 1970s it ran out of steam. Instead of a western-styled democracy, Russia is now ruled by Vladimir Putin, an ex-KGB agent who has been in power for some twenty-five years.

# Chapter One

# The One-Legged Chief

M I6 was formed in 1909 as an offshoot of foreign intelligence service to Vincent Kell's MI5 (home intelligence). During the First World War it managed to establish agents in Germany and Belgium, who reported back some valuable intelligence data. Captain Mansfield Cumming was installed at 2 Whitehall Court in Westminster – not just his headquarters, but also his home. At various times between 1911 and 1922, flats 53 and 54 on the seventh floor served as the Foreign Section of the Secret Service Bureau. Cumming constantly had to fight for funds for his service. Again and again, his officers had to pay agents and expenses out of their own pockets until later reimbursed. The accounts department was minutely scrutinised by Cumming's paymaster, known simply as 'Pay', and was notably examined for any wayward costs.

During the early years of his office, Cumming loved dressing up, disguising himself with a toupee, fake moustache and embellishment in a fashion he describes as 'rather peculiar.' He hired his clothes from William Berry Clarkson, a theatrical costume shop off Cambridge Circus, and entertained his 'top mates' by pretending to be a heavily-built German businessman.

A tragedy struck Mansfield Cumming just after war was declared in 1914. His son, Alastair, was driving Cumming's Rolls Royce – with Cumming in the passenger seat – at speed in northern France when a tyre blew and he lost control, crashing into a tree. He was thrown out of the vehicle, landed on his head and lingered on for several hours before dying. His father was pinned by the car and suffered two broken legs and an almost severed foot. It is reported that he used a sharp knife to cut away the foot and was able to crawl towards his son and wrapped Alastair in his coat. They were found some hours later; the father badly injured and his son dying. Cumming was operated on and made a surprisingly swift recovery. He was fitted with a wooden leg and one of his agents, Edward Knoblock, recalled that Cumming would terrify new recruits by grabbing a paper knife and suddenly stabbing his false leg. If the new recruit was dumbfounded, he would be dismissed as not being good enough to join the Intelligence Service.

William was born in 1859 in Lee, then in Kent, and his surname was Smith. His family founded the National Westminster Bank, so there was plenty of wealth around. He trained at Dartmouth from the age of 12, before being appointed a sub-lieutenant on HMS *Bellerophon*, fighting Malay pirates. He also served in the Egyptian War in 1884, during which the Egyptian army mutinied. He married May Cumming in 1889 and took her last name, which he incorporated with his own. Taking twelve years out of the Navy, he worked as an estate manager in Ireland until he returned to duty in 1898. He had a passion for speed and turned to the new sport of motor racing. He took part in driving a Wolseley in the Paris to Madrid race in May 1903. The roads were terrible, which resulted in eight people dead, including three spectators. He became a founding member of the Royal Aero Club in 1906 and he qualified as a pilot in 1913 at the age of 54. As if the speed of cars and airplanes hadn't been enough, Cumming owned a series of speedboats as well, which he also raced.

For a seaman, seasickness marred his naval career and he took semi-retirement. He spent a decade at Southampton developing boom defences and other special duties. Nearing retirement age, he received a letter dated 10 August 1909, from Rear Admiral Alexander Bethell, Director of Naval Intelligence, which read: 'Boom defence must be getting a bit stale. I have something good I can offer you and if you would like to come and see me on Thursday about noon, I will tell you what it is.'

Instead of having the Army and Navy intelligence services dealing with military matters, the government decided on an entirely new organisation called the Secret Service Bureau, with two separate divisions; one for domestic intelligence and the other covering countries abroad. Cumming was to be put in charge of the latter, gathering political, military and technical intelligence that if revealed, could endanger Britain. Cumming's first day at work on 7 October 1909 did not begin well. He recalled, 'Went to the office, and remained all day but saw no one, nor was there anything to do.' Cumming was so uninterested in his new post that he refused it and continued his work on the boom defence work at Southampton. Belatedly, he accepted the new post and wrote to Admiral Bethell, explaining that he 'had done nothing up to the present date except sit in the Office and I have received one letter containing my pay.'

It was all he could do to get permission from the War Office to purchase a cheap typewriter. This went on for a while before Cumming stirred himself and began to recruit agents and office staff. He called his staff 'top mates' and his agents 'rascals' and 'scallywags'. His role was reduced to gathering naval intelligence from Europe. This was something the Naval Intelligence Department (NID) could do with greater success and the NID proved to be the forerunner of the Government Communications Headquarters (GCHQ).

At the beginning of the First World War he had his first meeting with a foreign agent named Byzewski, who produced some useful intelligence on German shipbuilding. As Cumming did not speak German, they spent the whole of the interview flicking through the pages of an English-German phrase dictionary before Cumming realised that they could both speak French, and another meeting was hastily arranged. Among his agents were several authors, including Compton Mackenzie, Somerset Maugham and Valentine Williams. The rest of his agents were a mixed bunch; many of them a step away from criminality. Cumming wrote; 'All my staff are blackguards – but they are incapable ones, and a man with a little ingenuity and brains would be a change, even if not an agreeable one.'

Short of being a master spy, Cumming was accompanied by his assistant, Major Cyrus Regnart, to Brussels to meet an agent. Looking for somewhere quiet, they booked into a brothel and told the madam they were expecting another man to join them. The madam assumed they were homosexuals and dismissed them from her brothel before the police arrived.

During the First World War, he sent his agents to seek out troop and naval movements in Germany and Belgium, and built up a comprehensive intelligence library. His intelligence group had expanded and he had recruited some 1,000 agents working throughout Europe, and had more than sixty secretaries, typists and technical staff working at Whitehall Court. He reacted angrily at the interference of George Macdonogh (Director of Military Intelligence at the War Office, which dealt with purely military intelligence). Cumming was supported by Charles Hardinge, (Permanent Under-Secretary at the Foreign Office) who saw off Macdonogh's attempt to take over from Cumming, who was 'master of his own house.' Cumming responded by saying, 'Ever since the war started, my Bureau has been subjected to attacks which have disorganised and almost destroyed it ... The short-sighted actions of the War Office had already compromised his work in a number of countries, including Russia.' From the start, Cumming was sidelined by the Military Intelligence Directorate under the control of the Army and was not even allowed to read the War Office files.

Sir Mansfield Cumming was the first Chief of the Foreign Section of the Secret Service Bureau – later the Secret Intelligence Service - from 1909 until his death in 1923. He was a colourful character who had a penchant for attractive girls, speed and pornography. Among the things he bequeathed was his habit of initialling papers 'C' in green ink. This influence is still used today, as each subsequent chief of the service has adopted the pseudonym 'C'. This tradition inspired Ian Fleming to name James Bond's fictitious spymaster 'M'. At the beginning of the First World War, he was able to establish an organisation comprising of 1,000 staff, including posts in Buenos Aries, Cairo and Tokyo, but they did not expose any worthwhile intelligence secrets. It was not until 1917–18 that his department finally made a breakthrough. During the war, it lagged behind the rest of the secret service groups, but by the end of the war it produced a major coup.

Cumming recruited agents to work across the world and was engrossed by what became known as tradecraft – secret writing, disguises, inventions and mechanical gadgets, which he trialled in his own lab. During the First World War, Cumming was responsible for creating the wartime network 'La Dame Blanche', which was a Belgian group that reported on enemy troop movements. His opposite intelligence group, run by Captain Vernon Kell, was showered with agents and resources and by 1916 it was referred to as MI5. As the war rumbled on, Cumming was rebuffed by the Foreign Office, who refused him access to information from embassy officials and insisted that he did not gather intelligence about political developments abroad, for that was their job. Sir Samuel Hoare, the head of Petrograd station from May 1916 to May 1917, described Cumming as, 'jovial and very human, bluff and plain speaking, outwardly at least, a very simple man. In all respects, physical and mental, he was the very antithesis of the spy king of popular fiction.'

But by 1918, Special Intelligence Bureau (MI6) included 400 agents and was aided by the arrest of a number of German spies in England. With the British Embassy closed in Russia and all the agents deported, Cumming only had one agent, a musician with next to nothing in tradecraft but a fluency in Russian and a flair for disguise. An English Heritage blue plaque to Mansfield Cumming is at 2 Whitehall Court in Westminster, and at various times between 1911 and 1922, flats 53 and 54 – on the building's seventh floor – served not just as Cumming's home, but as the headquarters of the Foreign Section of the Secret Service Bureau. Today the exuberant nineteenth century French Renaissance-style building is grade II listed, and is part of The Royal Horse Guards Hotel, which overlooks the River Thames.

Following Paul Dukes, Cumming's finest agent was a Russian mole by the name of Boris Bazhanov. He was born and brought up in Ukraine, in the territory that was fought over continuously during the Ukrainian Civil War. He became a Soviet secretary of the Secretariat of the Communist Party of the Soviet Union, from which he later defected on 1 January 1928. Bazhanov was the personal secretary of Soviet leader Joseph Stalin from August 1923 to 1925 and held several prominent secretarial positions in the Politburo. Bazhanov was the only member of Stalin's Secretariat to defect and one of the first major subversive from the Eastern Block. Bazhanov defected the same year as the first of Stalin's five-year plans for the National Economy of the Soviet Union was accepted, avoiding the first purges that led up to the Great Purges of the mid-to-late 1930s. Bazhanov escaped south to Iran but later crossed the border into India and eventually sought safety in France. Over the years he survived several assassination attempts, and died at the age of 82 in Paris.

# Chapter Two

# The Death of Captain Francis Cromie

From 1909 and through the First World War the Intelligence Service had a variety of names, including Foreign Intelligence Service, the Secret Service, MI 1(c), the Special Intelligence Service and even 'C's Organisation. In May 1917 Captain Francis Newton Allen Cromie was appointed the *de facto* chief of the British Naval Intelligence Division operating in northern Russia. As naval attaché in the British Embassy in Petrograd, he was joined by a group of intelligence officers working throughout Russia, including Robert Bruce Lockhart, Samuel Hoare, John Scale, Cudbert Thornhill, Sidney Reilly, George Alexander Hill, Oswald Rayner and Stephen Alley. Arthur Ransome, a left-wing journalist reporting for the *Daily News* who was also working for MI6, was a particular friend of his; he said of Cromie; 'No man more noble or constant, who was a true friend of Russia as he was one of the few capable of inspiring trust on both sides of the ever-widening divide.'

Cromie had been captain on the new submarine HMS *K19* and had taken over command of the Baltic Flotilla from Commander Max Horton in 1915. His record was impressive. As a cadet teenager, he fought with the Naval Brigade against the Boxers in China in 1900 and received the China War Medal. Entering Beijing, he fought alongside Austria's submarine hero Lieutenant Georg Ritter von Trapp, father of the famous Von Trapp singers who later gained fame as the family *The Sound of Music* was based on.

Cromie was one of the first officers to command a submarine, the *A3* in 1906. While in command, he received the Royal Humane Society's Bronze Medal for risking his own life trying to save a drowning sailor in the Channel. He served in the Baltic, where he suspended German maritime traffic in the area. During this time he sank five ships and gave pause to the Swedes for shipping iron ore to Germany. He later torpedoed a German destroyer and sank the German cruiser *Undine*, for which he was decorated with the Order of St George by the tsar, the Legion of

Honour by the French, and a British Distinguished Service Order. When he was killed, he was posthumously appointed a Companion of the Order of the Bath.

Cromie could have come home with his men but decided to stay behind in Russia. As most of the senior staff had vacated the embassy in Petrograd, Cromie was designated Naval Attaché and took over as *de facto* representative of the crown. However, his real reason for remaining was his love affair with Sonia Gagarin, a beautiful socialite. Cromie was described as a raconteur and a mediator; he was fluent in Russian, and he was well respected by the Tsarists and many of the Bolsheviks. He was also a skilled watercolour artist, a lover, a teetotal and a non-smoker. Among his associates were Sidney Reilly, Robert Bruce Lockhart and – surprisingly – Lenin and Trotsky. Cromie stayed behind when most of the embassy staff returned to London and helped many expatriates to escape from the Bolsheviks.

On 14 August the head Cheka, Felix Dzerzhinsky, decided to infiltrate Cromie's intelligence unit. He sent along one of his agents, Jan Buikis, to make contact with Cromie. In a meeting together with Boyce, Lockhart, Sidney Reilly and Colonel Berzin, commander of the Lettish battalion, it was agreed to finance an anti-Bolshevik coup. To their horror, the 1,200,000 roubles handed over to Berzin were handed straight to the Bolsheviks.

By 31 August Felix Dzerzhinsky had ordered that all agents in the British Embassy were to be rounded up and imprisoned. There were vehicles drawing up in the courtyard and a lot of commotion. Cromie looked out of the window and saw the Cheka and some patrol boats that had moved up the canal in front of the embassy with their guns trained on the building. They had learnt of allied plans to land troops at Murmansk and Archangel in an attempt to unseat Lenin. Cromie had also arranged an appointment with agent Sidney Reilly but their date was interrupted by a meeting. Reilly decided to go to the Embassy, having waited for fifteen minutes for Cromie. The meeting at the embassy included Cromie, Harold Hall of MI6, and Colonel Steckelmann and Sabir, who were double agents while claiming to be officers of the White Russians. They were – in reality – members of the Cheka, who took over the British Embassy.

About 4.50 pm, staff in the embassy heard shouts: the Cheka had arrived. (Its full title was the All-Russian Extraordinary Commission for

Combating Counter-Revolution and Sabotage – something of a mouth full). Hearing the disturbance outside, Cromie told his guests to remain inside the room. He drew a pistol, opened the door and surprised a Cheka officer who was opening the doors in the corridor. Aiming his pistol at the Cheka officer, he called out, 'Get back, you swine!' and drove him back to the ornamental staircase. He saw some Cheka soldiers come through the doorway and fired at them. He turned down the staircase with the Cheka officer shielding him, taking two steps at a time as the Cheka came into the ground floor. They fired wildly with the bullets hitting the balustrade, missing Cromie but wounding the Cheka officer.

One of the remaining embassy staff was Nathalie Bucknell, who worked in the passport office. It was exactly 4.50 pm when she heard the sound of gunfire coming from upstairs. She poked her head around the doorway and heard a terrible scream. The embassy porter signalled to her to take cover and she crouched in a small alcove adjoining the hall. She heard a group of men rushing down the marble staircase in pursuit of Francis Cromie. He was firing his revolver at the rest of the Cheka who were coming through the entrance. The crackle of gunfire increased as the shoot-out intensified and the bullets began to ricochet off the marble walls and columns. As Cromie reached the last step, he paused and then fell backwards, having been shot in the head by the men who had ransacked the upstairs offices. The Red Guards rushed past Cromie's body and into the street, looking for their backup. Still coming down the stairs were more Red Guards and one of them aimed a kick at the stricken Cromie. Nathalie heard shouts from the Cheka ordering the staff to come out of their rooms or they would open fire.

The Reverend Bousfield Swan Lombard, chaplain to the embassy, saw Cromie's body and tried to help but the Cheka pulled him away. Nathalie ran to Cromie and was joined by Miss Myrna Blumberg as they knelt beside the fatally wounded officer. She saw that his 'eyelids and lips moved very faintly'. A group of Red Guards appeared and pointed their weapons at the two ladies and ordered them upstairs. Not daring to argue, they were hustled upstairs where they saw evidence of the shoot-out, with blood and shells littering the floor. They were pushed into the Chancery room, where Ernest Boyce (head of Mansfield Cumming's Petrograd MI6) and Robert Bruce Lockhart (Head of Chancery) were held at gunpoint.

The room became full of Red Guards, who ordered the porter to unlock the doors and cupboards in all the offices. The hostages were held for several hours while the embassy was stripped of everything of value, including secret documents. Then the staff were marched downstairs and out into the street, passing Francis Cromie's body on the pavement. They were taken to the Peter and Paul Fortress, where they were interrogated for fifteen hours. Nathalie heard one of the soldiers say they were going to execute Ernest Boyce, Robert Bruce Lockhart and three others but this was cancelled due to a last-minute prisoner swap. At 11.00 am the following day they were told they were free to return to England.

Sidney Reilly reached the end of Vlademirovsky Prospect and saw that the embassy door had been torn from its hinges, and the flag had been torn down. On the pavement were several bloodstained Cheka corpses who had been shot while trying to storm the building. A military car sped by, filled with Red Guards ready to invade the British Embassy. Pedestrians scattered, diving into doorways and side streets to avoid being caught up in the invasion of the the British Embassy. It would be hours before he found out what had happened at the embassy. The Danish government informed Britain that Captain Cromie had been murdered while trying to prevent the Bolsheviks from entering the embassy. He had killed three soldiers before being shot in the back of the head. His decoration, Cross of St George, was grabbed from his breast and worn by one of his murderers.

An account appeared in Mary Britieva's 1934 book, *One Woman's Story*. She served as a nurse on the Eastern Front and recounts the events witnessed by her sister-in-law, Nathalie Bucknell, in the embassy.

My sister-in-law ran into the hallway and as she emerged she saw Captain Cromie running down the steps, two at a time, straight towards her. Behind him at the top of the stairs stood a man firing at the Captain. Several bullets whizzed past her head and crashed through the glass of the entrance doors behind her. Her horror seemed to root her to the spot and suddenly, just as Captain Cromie reached the last stair, he pitched forward as if he had stumbled, staggered a little and then crashed down backwards with his head on the bottom step. My sister (Nathalie) ran to him and lifted his head. He was moving his eyelids and she felt something warm trickling down the fingers of her right hand with which she was holding up his head from underneath. Suddenly a terrific blow made her drop Captain Cromie's head and sent her spinning against the right hand wall. The man who had struck her grabbed her and ran up the stairs hitting her violently from time to time and finally pushing her into the Chancery room where she found all the members of the Embassy and the Consulate standing with hands raised above their heads. After being searched for arms, the Embassy staff were forced to hand over their papers and then marched downstairs and on to the street.

Francis Cromie's body had been taken upstairs and hurled from a window into the street. Had the shot not killed him, then the fall from the second-floor window surely would have. His body was carried to an undertaker and placed in a coffin. The small cortege passed along the banks of the Neva where several destroyers were moored. On board, the slovenly revolutionary sailors stirred themselves, formed in ranks and gave him a final salute to a fellow sailor. His body was either taken to Archangel and buried in the Lutheran cemetery, or interred in Petrograd's Smolensk Cemetery without a gravestone. The War Cabinet in England issued a warning to the Bolsheviks that if any harm came to British subjects, 'His Majesty's Government will hold the members of the Soviet Government individually responsible, and will make every endeavour to secure that they shall be treated as outlaws by the governments of all civilized nations, and that no place of refuge shall be left to them.'

The Bolshevik newspaper, *Pravda*, pointed the finger at Lockhart, who was languishing in the Lubyanka Prison in Moscow. 'Ten million roubles assigned for this purpose, Lockhart entered into personal contact with the commander of a large Lettish unit should the plot succeed, Lockhart promised in the name of the Allies immediate restoration of a free Latvia … Anglo-French capitalists, through hired assassins, organised terrorist attempts on representatives of the Soviet.'

The Red Terror was the period of political opression and mass murder carried out by the Bolsheviks in the years 1917–1922. It was a time of dreadful killings and famine, which actually extended into the 1930s. Throughout Petrograd, the citizens thought of two subjects that were of overwhelming interest – food and the Cheka; to procure the one and avoid the other. On 3 March 1918, the Treaty of Brest-Litovsk was signed, ending Russia's participation in the war. One of the conditions was that Cromie's five submarines were to be surrendered to the Germans. Instead, they were sunk in the Baltic Sea. It also meant that Russia had to cede the province of Kars Oblast to the Ottoman Empire and recognise the independence of Ukraine.

In 1909, Bruce Lockhart was sent to Malaya to train as a rubber planter. While there, he fell in love with Amai, a young Malay princess, and installed her in his colonial bungalow. They embarked on a torrid affair which resulted in hostility among the Malays. He and his lover received death threats and Lockhart was eventually smuggled out of Malaya and was forced to abandon his lover to an uncertain fate. He returned to London and became a civil servant. By 1912, he had been appointed Vice-Chancellor in Moscow, where he shone. Giles Milton, the author of *Russian Roulette*, wrote:

> On the face of it, Lockhart was well suited to the job for which he had been appointed. He spoke good Russian and had previously served as Consul General in Moscow. Thirty years of age and in the prime of life, he was affable, colourful and endlessly entertaining … Lockhart had many failings and he wrote about them with disarming honesty. His lack of discretion would have been a handicap in any employment but it was doubly alarming in a diplomat. His appetite for women was another drawback.

On 28 February 1918 the British Embassies in Petrograd and Moscow were evacuated, and diplomatic representation was left in the hands of Robert Bruce Lockhart, the acting Consular-General. The ambassador, Sir George Buchanan, was outraged at being removed, thinking he should have taken charge of the agents left behind. Lockhart had the more secretive job of organising the functions of the British spies who had been sent by Mansfield Cumming, the head of SIS, to collect information of Bolshevik intrigue. They were Sidney Reilly, George Alexander Hill, Cudbert Thornhill, Ernest Boyce, Oswald Raynor, Stephen Alley, and Harold Hall.

On 17 August 1918, Reilly travelled from Moscow to Petrograd and arrived at the moment that Moisei Uritsky was assassinated. A young cadet named Leonid Kannegisser sat in the crowded waiting room of the Cheka headquarters, anxiously waiting for the head of the Petrograd Cheka to arrive. He was the 24-year-old son of a millionaire and an amateur poet. He had been a supporter of Kerensky but had progressed to anti-Bolshevik views with links to the White Russian counter-revolutionary groups. Moisei Uritsky had played a prominent role in organising the Revolution. He was a member of the Central Committee of the Bolshevik Party and oversaw the Petrograd secret police. He arrived in a chauffeur-driven car and entered the building. He passed Kannegisser, who stood up and pulled out his gun and fired into the back of Uritsky, hitting him in the body and head. The onlookers screamed and were rooted to the spot as Uritsky fell dead. Kannegisser ran outside to his bicycle and pedalled furiously away. In the panic, the Cheka guards opened fire – not very accurately – as the young cadet sped around the Winter Palace and along the Neva Embankment, into Millionnaya Street. He lost his cap, which was picked up by one of the guards. According to Kannegisser's testimony, he ditched his bike and ran into the courtyard of Number 17. He somehow managed to find an overcoat which he thought would disguise him, but to no avail. He was soon arrested and taken back to Cheka headquarters, where his fate was a foregone conclusion and he was executed by a bullet in the back of the head.

Added to this, on 30 August Lenin was shot and badly wounded. A Socialist Revolutionary named Fania Kaplan confessed to the assassination attempt. She was an anarchist who had spent eleven years in a Siberian labour camp, which badly affected her health. As a result, Kaplan suffered from continuous headaches, deafness and periods of blindness. She went to a factory where Lenin was delivering a rallying speech to the workers. As Lenin approached his car at about 10.00 pm, the light was quite bad. A crowd gathered around to cheer him on his way. The story goes that Kaplan stood at the back of the crowd, carrying a briefcase and umbrella – which would have hampered any attempt to assassinate Lenin. It is unlikely she would have been able to kill him, given her partial blindness. The gunfire panicked the crowd and the Red Guards rounded up those they had caught. Kaplan was not one of them. In a poor state of health, she stood on a couch and confessed that she had killed Lenin. She later made the following statement at Cheka headquarters.

My name is Fania Kaplan. Today I shot at Lenin. I did it on my own. I will not say from whom I obtained my revolver. I will give no details. I had resolved to kill Lenin long ago. I consider him a traitor to the Revolution. I was exiled to Akatui for participating in an assassination attempt against a Tsarist official in Kiev. I spent eleven years at hard labour. After the Revolution, I was freed. I favoured the Constituent Assembly and am still for it.

When it became clear that Kaplan would not implicate any accomplices, she was executed on 3 September 1918. In fact, an unknown gunman had shot Lenin and quite why Fania Kaplan confessed is not known. Although Lenin was not expected to live, he rallied and managed to recover, but he began to be plagued by a series of strokes which eventually led to his death in 1924. This put a stop to the British agents' plans of a coup. As a reprisal, the Bolsheviks began mass arrests, interrogations and executions, mostly within their own members. There was some suggestion that the murder was planned by some members of the Bolshevik Party. The Commissars for Justice and Internal Affairs issued a decree on 5 September.

In the given situation it is absolutely essential to safeguard the rear by means of terror … it is essential to protect the Soviet Republic against its class enemies by isolating those in concentration camps; plots and insurrections are to be shot. It is an open licence for the Cheka to kill.

The assassination of Uritsky, the attempted murder of Lenin and the killing of Francis Cromie marked the beginning of that period of history known as the Red Terror. Robert Bruce Lockhart continued with his plans to overthrow the Bolshevik government via Colonel Eduard Berzin, who reported that his 10,000 Lettish (Latvian) troops had lost all enthusiasm for protecting the Bolsheviks and wanted to return home. George Alexander Hill wrote that: 'The Letts were the corner stone and foundation of the Soviet government. They guarded the Kremlin, gold stocks and munitions … They occupied many other positions of consequence, including at the head of the Extraordinary Commissions (Cheka), the prisons, the banks and the railroads were Letts.' Lockhart was sceptical of the Letts and said: 'The Letts are Bolshevik servants because they have no other resort. They are foreign hirelings serving for money. They are at the disposal of the highest bidder.'

In fact, Berzin was a spy for the Bolsheviks but his efforts at exposing the British agents came to naught. He was promoted to the Far North Construction Trust, known as Dalstroy. These were Siberian camps where prisoners were sent to build roads and mine for gold in a vast, empty region called Kolyma, bedevilled by mosquitoes in the summer and sub-zero temperatures in the winter. He became head of the Magadan, which forced prisoners to work the gold-fields and later he ran the labour camps in Siberia. During the Great Purge of 1936–38, as part of Stalin's plan to remove men who could take over his position, Berzin was arrested. On 19 December 1937 he was incarcerated, put on trial and on 1 August 1938 was executed in Lubyanka Prison.

On 31 August, Lockhart was awakened by the Cheka at 3.30 am, and he later recalled; 'As I opened my eyes, I looked up into the steely barrel of a revolver. There were some ten men in my room.' He was taken to Lubyanka Prison, where he was interrogated by Yakov Peters, Dzerzhinsky's Cheka deputy.

> At the table, with a revolver lying beside the writing pad, was a man dressed in black trousers and a white Russian shirt... His lips were tightly compressed and, as I entered the room, his eyes fixed me with a steely stare. His face was sallow and sickly, as if he never saw the light of day.

Peters asked if Lockhart knew Fania Kaplan, who had shot and badly wounded Lenin on 31 August. Lockhart denied having heard of her. He was thoroughly interrogated about British involvement in an attempt to overthrow the Bolshevik government, which Lockhart also denied. He was asked about Sidney Reilly but declined all knowledge of him as well. He was taken back to his cell and at 6.00 am was joined by a black-haired woman with dark rings under her eyes. This was the would-be assassin, Fania Kaplan, who was taken away and executed a few hours later. Lockhart described his cell.

> My prison here consists of a small hall, a sitting-room, a diminutive bedroom, a bathroom and a small dressing-room, which I use for my food. The rooms open on both sides on to corridors so that there is

no fresh air. I have one sentry one side and two on the other. They are changed every four hours and as each change has to come in to see if I am there. This results in my being woken up at twelve or four in the middle of the night.

Despite the evidence against him, Peters released Lockhart. The British government had secretly arranged for Lockhart and other British agents to be exchanged for Maxim Litinov and several Soviet officials on 2 October 1918. The organisation's cover was blown. Lockhart returned to England and worked in the Foreign Office before moving to banking. He joined the Central European Bank that was run by the Bank of England. In 1932 he wrote a best-selling book entitled *Memoirs of a British Agent*. During the Second World War he served as Director General of the Political Warfare Executive, responsible for coordinating all propaganda against the Axis powers. After the war he became close friends with Ian Fleming and relayed stories of his adventures and others he knew about. Lockhart published many books on spying, politics, the military and whiskey. He lived until he was 82 and died in 1970.

The Cheka, or the Extraordinary Commission, became the strongest civil institution in Russia and there are many instances when it overrode the decrees of the central government. A prominent instance was the execution of four former grand dukes, Paul Alexandrovich, George Michailovich, Nicholas Mihailovich and Dmitri Konstantinovich in the summer of 1919. The four were cousins of the tsar and they were executed in Peter and Paul Fortress in Petrograd, on orders of the Extraordinary Commission. Instead of the government putting them on trial, the Cheka went straight ahead and shot them, then buried them in a common grave by a party of Lettish and Chinese soldiers.

# Chapter Three

# The Agents

## Sidney Reilly

Georgi Rosenblum was born in 1873, the only son of Hersh Yakov Rozenblium and his wife Paulina. Brought up in Odessa, he left his home in his teenage years. His parents converted to Catholicism, a move that was highly unusual. He spun many tales about how he had been a cook, a dockworker, a railway engineer and a brothel doorman in Brazil. He also claimed that he attended Heidelberg and Cambridge universities, as well as the Royal School of Mines. He managed to gain sufficient knowledge to be accepted by the Institute of Chemistry Society in 1897. He also had an ear for languages and could easily call upon English, French, Russian, German and Polish. His early life is a mystery, but in 1899 he called himself Sidney Reilly and had the passport to prove his name. With his strong Jewish features and accented English, Reilly proved to be an unconvincing Englishman, although his grasp of English was exceptional. According to author Brian Marriner, he *possessed passports in eleven different names.'* He possessed great charm which captivated women and he was never without a string of mistresses.

During the Boer War, he pretended to be a Russian arms dealer and gave the British intelligence information about Dutch arms shipments to the Boers. During the Russo-Japanese War in 1904, he also obtained information on Russian defences in Manchuria for the Japanese secret police. He involved himself with many fake businesses, including the Ozone Preparations Company, which peddled patent medicines. He also became a paid informant for the organisation that was filled with suspected Russian anarchists. In 1896 Reilly joined the émigré intelligence network run by William Melville, the Superintendent of Scotland Yard's Special Branch. Melville went on to become the first head of the Secret Service Bureau. Reilly was employed by the Special Branch. He later joined the

Foreign Section of the British Secret Service Bureau and it was here he met Mansfield Cumming.

Reilly and another agent were at the Frankfurt International Air Show in 1909 and wanted to get hold of a new magneto which was far ahead of its rivals. According to Bruce Lockhart, the new German aeroplane lost control and crashed, killing the pilot. Reilly and a fellow agent posed as the exhibition pilots, removed the magneto and substituted it with another. They hurriedly made detailed drawings and when the aircraft was removed to a hangar, they restored the original magneto.

Reilly seemed to be everywhere. He managed to apply to become a welder in the Krupp armaments factory, where he stole weapon information for the Allies. It was rumoured that he killed two night watchmen while stealing the plans. The German naval ship builders employed him before the First World War and he was able to pass blueprints and specifications to SIS. With the outbreak of war, he went to New York as a war contractor, buying arms for the Russians. He kept in contact with Mansfield Cumming, and in 1917 he managed to enter Germany to discover how close the country was to defeat. Norman Thwaites, an ex-journalist, described him as a con man:

> Having a swarthy complexion, a long straight nose, piercing eyes, black hair brushed back from a forehead suggesting keen intelligence, a large mouth and figure slight and medium height. Always clothed immaculately, he was a man that impressed one with a sense of power … Not only had he charming manners, but he was a most agreeable companion with a fund of information in many spheres.

Reilly returned to England and joined the Royal Flying Corps as a second lieutenant but it is not known if he flew. According to Robin Bruce Lockhart in his book *Ace of Spies*, 'Reilly was dropped by plane behind enemy lines, sometimes in Belgium, sometimes in Germany, sometimes disguised as a peasant, sometimes as a German officer or soldier, when he usually carried forged papers to indicate he had been wounded and was on sick-leave from the front. In this way he was able to move throughout Germany with complete freedom.' Thwaites told John Scale that Reilly would make a good agent inside Russia, although some of the other agents were wary of him. He had a flair for intelligence work and was admired by both Mansfield Cumming and Winston Churchill.

The former sent Reilly to Russia in 1918, where he joined the conspiracy led by Robert Bruce Lockhart. The main objective was to overthrow the Bolshevik government. Reilly had a passionate hatred of communism and declared: 'Bolshevism has been baptised in the blood of the bourgeois. Its leaders are criminals, assassins, murderers, gunmen, desperadoes. Over all, silent, secret, ferocious, menacing hung the crimson shadow of Cheka. The new masters were ruling Russia.' He was not always favoured by his fellow agents, however, and one said that Reilly 'has made money since the beginning of the war through influence with corrupted members of the Russian purchasing commissions ... and we consider him untrustworthy and unsuitable to work suggested.' Another agent said that 'Reilly was a shrewd businessman of undoubted ability but without patriotism or principles and therefore not recommended for any position which requires loyalty as he would not hesitate to use it to further his own commercial interests.'

Reilly began perfecting several different personas; the two he most favoured were a Levantine merchant named Konstantine Markovich Massino and a Greek businessman named Constantine. He joined a Bolshevik Liquidation Society made up of other agents that met to discuss how to eliminate the top men. In April 1918 he joined the intelligence team in Petrograd and Moscow under the Head of Special Mission to the Soviet Government, Robert Bruce Lockhart, with the rank of consul general. By the end of August, Francis Cromie had been killed in retaliation for the murder of Moise Uritsky, and the blame fell on the British. The Cheka had the staff of the British Embassy imprisoned, including some of the agents. Reilly had seen the final shootout from outside the building and immediately went into hiding. He paid 60,000 roubles to be smuggled out of Petrograd on board a Dutch freighter. He arrived back in London with George Hill and both men went to see Mansfield Cumming who immediately awarded them the Military Cross. They were fully expecting to take it easy for a few weeks but Cumming had other plans, and they were told that they had two hours to catch a train that would take them to Odessa.

From December 1918 to March 1919 he was able to send intelligence from Southern Russia. In 1925 he was arrested and thoroughly interrogated. It is not known if he divulged any secrets but he was taken to a wooded district outside Moscow and shot, although some maintained he was alive during the Second World War.

Sidney Reilly was considered an outstanding agent but he did have some foibles, including gambling and a visceral hatred of Bolshevism. One of the plots he was involved in was the assassination of Uritsky, for which Leonid Kannegisser paid with his life. In 1924 he even managed to smuggle the infamous Zinoviev letter into England. He travelled in and out of Russia for eight years before he was arrested. Thanks to Robert Bruce Lockhart's 1932 bestselling book, *Memoirs of a British Agent*, the world press focused of Sidney Reilly and he became a famous spy with his many espionage adventures. He was dubbed by the newspapers as 'the greatest spy in history' and 'the Scarlet Pimpernel of Red Russia'.

## George Alexander Hill

George Alexander Hill was born in Estonia in 1892. He was the son of a timber merchant, who accompanied his father on trips to the Caspian Sea and Persia. He was fishing in northern British Columbia when the First World War broke out and he applied to join the Canadian army. He was taken on by Princess Patricia's Canadian Light Infantry and later was commissioned. He had a natural ear for languages and besides Russian, he could speak six languages, including French and German. 'I had half a dozen languages at the tip of my tongue and learned to sum up the characteristic qualities and faults of a dozen nationalities.'

In April 1915 his skill at mastering German meant that he was sent out to no man's land from the frontline at St Julien on the Ypres battlefront to gather intelligence. He wrote in his book *Go Spy the Land*:

> Owing to my languages, I found myself a full-blown interpreter as soon as we arrived in France … but I was thoroughly interested in the examination of prisoners and their documents, the taking down of their statements, and from little pieces of information building up, as one does, a jigsaw puzzle, a complete picture.
>
> Early in April we moved up to the Ypres front and I was put entirely on Intelligence work. About the middle of the month our division took up a position around St Julien. We were expecting some sort of an attack at any time, and it was most important for

us to know whether the enemy were getting any reinforcements. As my knowledge of German was exceptional, night after night I slipped out between the lines to listen to the German troops in their trenches. One could tell by the accent whether the soldiers were Bavarians or Saxons ...

It was a nerve-racking business wandering through no-man's-land, and horrible because for months there had been intermittent fighting all around the sodden, reeking, clay fields over which I crawled. One night as I crept through the pitch dark my right hand touched something, and, with a sickening squish, sank through. It was the body of a poor fellow who had been lying there for weeks.

On another night, when I was close to the German trenches, I was challenged, and the challenge was followed by a hand grenade. The result was a shattered kneecap.

A few weeks later he received his commission and was transferred to a post on the Intelligence Staff at the War Office. He was asked if he could speak Russian, but the authorities had other plans and he had to attend a crammer and learn Bulgarian in four weeks. Besides learning a new language, he was also taught how to recognise the signs of being shadowed, and had to learn a system of codes and other means of dodges which were useful to spies. He was later sent to the Balkan city of Monastir, where he witnessed the execution of two Bulgarian spies. He left a graphic description of them being killed by a firing squad.

The wall behind, white a moment before, was scarred by bullet marks and bespattered with blood, just as if a paint brush had been dipped into a pot of red paint and flicked on the wall ... I hurried off to find a spot where I could be sick without disgracing myself.

Sent to Salonika as an intelligence officer attached to XII Corps, he formed a spy network. In the hot, humid Balkans (Serbia, Greece, Bulgaria) he soon caught malaria and was hospitalised. He spent a fortnight in a hospital in Salonika before being regulated to desk duties. Hating the routine, he applied for flying lessons and became a fully-fledged pilot with the Royal Flying Corps. His job was to take agents by a BE2e aeroplane and drop them behind enemy lines. Once, when he took Petrov – one of his best spies – to a spot, the engine cut out after landing. Hill and Petrov tried to get the engine to fire again but to no avail. Both were covered in sweat from the exertion and in the distance they saw an enemy cavalry patrol approaching.

> Petrov said that he would have one more swing, but before doing so we decided to release the carrier pigeons. We had instructions in the event of a likely capture immediately to get rid of the pigeons, so that the enemy could not use them to send information calculated to mislead our Intelligence department. Off flew the four pigeons. And then like a demon possessed, Petrov started swinging the propeller. Still nothing happened.
>
> The cavalry patrol had spotted us. I think at first they thought it was one of their own machines. Then they must have got suspicious, for they started trotting over towards us. Suddenly the engine fired. Petrov raced round to the fuselage and leaped into his seat. The cavalry patrol broke into a gallop and called on us to stop. I opened up the throttle and we were away, but before we had left the ground the patrol opened fire. Their shooting was good, for we found when we got back to our aerodrome half a dozen bullet holes were in the fuselage.

In July 1917, Hill – code-named IK8 – was recruited by Mansfield Cumming and sent to Petrograd with the RFC mission in Russia. Hill used one of the codes while working as an agent in Russian. 'It had been invented by a genius at the Secret Service headquarters in London and the many I have seen it was the easiest and safest for a secret service man to carry.' He ran a string of couriers, some of whom were captured and executed. He changed the system and placed a former Russian cavalry officer named Agent Z in charge. Hill had nine other safe houses including a dacha outside Moscow. Agent Z rented rooms run by the widow of an officer killed in the war. She lived in the Bond Street of Moscow, Tverskaya Street, and worked as a high-class prostitute, which gave Agent Z the perfect cover. 'What was more natural than that unknown men should constantly be coming and going in and out of her flat ... and our weary couriers could rest in safety in one of our rooms there.'

He described living a double life: 'Part of the day I would be in uniform and living as a British officer, the rest of the time I was dressed in mufti, visiting my agents on foot. I was looking ahead and beginning to organise secret quarters which would be very necessary for me once the Bolsheviks attempted to restrict my activities.'

A tragedy occurred on 17 July 1918, eight months after the Revolution. The tsar's family had endeavoured to appeal to King George V to come to Britain. Although the British government agreed, George did not, mainly because Tsarina Alexandra was German. With Yekaterinburg under pressure from the White Russians, a firing squad took the royal family down to the cellar and executed them. News of this caused shock and outrage in Britain, and the Bolsheviks were classed as heinous criminals in the British government's eyes.

Hill worked for SIS in the Middle East for the next three years, but shortage of funds meant he was retired to live in a caravan in Sussex. He received not only the Military Cross but also an MBE and the DSO. He then sought employment with the Royal Dutch Shell Oil Company, then manager of the Globe Theatre in Shaftesbury Avenue and the deputy-manager to the impresario, C.B. Cochran. At the start of the Second World War he was called back to the SIS and worked as an instructor in Section D near Hertford, where one of his pupils was Kim Philby.

In 1940, he was selected to head an SOE mission to Moscow. He worked with the NKVD to coordinate sabotage and propaganda and to infiltrate agents into occupied Europe. When the war was over, Hill became a director of British-owned mineral water company *Apollinarius* – a strange vehicle for a man who liked his drink. He died in 1968 in London, shortly after his second marriage.

## Oswald Raynor

Born on 29 November 1888 in Smethick, Staffordshire, he was the son of Thomas Raynor, a draper. In 1907–1910 he studied modern languages at Oriel College, Oxford, where he met Felix Yusupov (Count Sumarokov-Elston). According to Richard Cullen, author of *Rasputin: The Role of Britain's Secret Service*, 'Their friendship lasted a lifetime ... one is drawn to conclude, given Yusupov's homosexual/bisexual tendencies, that he and Raynor may well have at sometime been sexually involved.'

Raynor left university and became a barrister in the Inner Temple. When war was declared, Raynor sought a commission in the British Army, but his fluency in languages was recognised as having intelligence potential.

He was commissioned in the Special List and assigned to Cumming. He learned ciphers and how to avoid being followed, until in December 1915 Cumming sent him to Russia. He joined other agents in the British Secret Intelligence Service under the leadership of Samuel Hoare. He became friendly with Vladimir Purishkevich and learned of a plot to kill Gregory Rasputin. He later recalled that Purishkevich's tone 'was so casual that I thought his words were symptomatic of what everyone was thinking and saying rather than the expression of a definitely thought-out plan.' A week later, on 7 January 1917, Stephen Ally wrote to John Scale in Romania, saying that Raynor would attend to 'loose ends and will no doubt brief you on your return.'

In 1918 Raynor was posted to Stockholm, where he served under John Scale. He recruited Russian speakers to infiltrate Russia. When he returned to Russia, he was sent to Vladivostok. He left the British Army in 1920 and took part in a trade mission to Moscow in 1921. In 1927 Raynor helped Yusupov with writing his account of the murder, which was pure fiction. After Raynor's death in 1961, the evidence pointed to the fact that he was with Yusupov at Rasputin's murder. Neither Vladimir Purishkevich nor Yusupov mention the close-quarters shot to the forehead. In fact, it was Raynor who had the Webley revolver that fired the last shot at Rasputin. He had been shot in the side, then later hit in the back before finally dying from a gunshot wound to the head.

In 1920 Raynor left the SIS and became the Finnish Foreign Correspondent for the *Daily Telegraph*. He had a son named John Felix Raynor, named after his close association Felix Yusupov. Raynor died at Botley, Surrey in 1961 and his son died not long after.

## Stephen Alley

Stephen Alley was born on 14 February 1876 in the House of Yusupov Palace in Moscow of all places. His father was an engineer employed on the project of railway construction in Russia. Alley grew up speaking fluent Russian and attended King's College London to study English Literature before moving to Glasgow, where he took a degree in engineering. He joined the family firm of Alley and McLellan Engineers and returned to Russia to help build the first heavy pipe line to the Black Sea. In 1914 he was recruited by Captain Archibald Wavell into the Secret Intelligence Bureau and described his first meeting with Mansfield Cumming.

'C' sent me to meet the Russian Military Attaché, Lieutenant General Nikolai Ermelov, who occupied a flat in the same building. The only remark 'C' made to me was I might not fit the job as I had not any decorations. A second interview with Ermelov apparently my knowledge of Russia made him agree to my appointment.

Alley was involved in the killing of Rasputin, who was promised that Prince Yusupov's wife would be in attendance. In fact, she was on holiday in the Crimea. According to *Six: A History of Britain's Secret Intelligence Service* by Michael Smith, once at Yusupov's Palace:

> Rasputin was plied with drink and then tortured in order to discover the truth of his alleged links with Germany's attempt to persuade Russia to leave the war. The torture was carried out with an astonishing level of violence, probably using a heavy rubber cosh – the original autopsy report found that his testicles had been crushed flat and there is more than a suspicion that the extent of the damage was fuelled by sexual jealousy … Whatever Rasputin actually told the conspirators, and someone in his predicament could be expected to say anything that might end the ordeal, they had no choice but to murder him and dispose of the body. He was shot several times, with three different weapons, with all evidence suggesting that Raynor fired the final shot, using his personal Webley revolver.

In February 1917 Samuel Hoare returned to London and handed over the reins to Stephen Alley. In his book *Secret Service: the Making of the British Intelligence Community*, Christopher Andrew stated that Alley had been dismissed from the Secret Intelligence Bureau by Cumming. He later revealed that he had been told to assassinate Joseph Stalin. 'I didn't always obey orders. Once I was asked to rub out Stalin. Never did like the chap much but the idea of walking into his office and killing him offended me.' Alley returned to London in March 1918 and was transferred to MI5. He died in Hertfordshire in 1969.

## Cudbert Thornhill

Cudbert Thornhill was born on 4 October 1883 in Tibet to a father who was a British Indian Army officer in charge of the British frontier station. He followed his father into the Indian Army and became fluent in Russian, French and Indian dialects. He came to the attention of Mansfield Cumming and was later recruited into MI6. In May 1915 he replaced the irascible Captain Archibald Campbell to be his representative in Petrograd. Thornhill was subordinate to Colonel Alfred Knox, the military attaché in Petrograd, and he got on well with him. Thornhill worked for Lieutenant Colonel Samuel Hoare, head of the SIS section of the Petrograd Embassy, and had been described as 'a first class Russian scholar and a good shot with rifle, catapult, shot-gun and blow-pipe.' It was noticeable that relations in the embassy improved in Petrograd.

In 1916, he was made assistant military attaché in control of military intelligence. A journalist who met him in Russia claimed that, 'Thornhill was one of the bravest men – and most silent – I have ever met. He was a calm, dignified, silent man, almost detached in his bearing, until the moment came for quick action; then the iciness would erupt like a volcano.'

One of his agents was Arthur Ransome, Russian correspondent for *The Daily News,* who was almost entirely left-wing but was a capable agent and ruffled the public's feathers. Thornhill confined himself strictly to his duties and proved to be a very good intelligence officer. He succeeded in placing the Mission on thoroughly good terms with the Embassy, and everything went perfectly smoothly. Over the next twelve months, relations between Cumming and Thornhill became strained, although the actual work was not clandestine. In 1916 he was transferred to the embassy and given special responsibility for 'enemy identification.'

In 1917 Thornhill and John Scale were sent to Romania to access the Russian Army's preparedness against a German attack. It was decided that they should dismantle Romania's oil fields to prevent the Germans making use of them. He returned to Petrograd during the Revolution, and according to one source, 'he was the hero of many exciting adventures during the revolution.' He was forced to go into hiding but by January 1918 he was back reporting that the new Red Army had been formed 'with munitions workers because they were considered more intelligent that peasants.'

He was appointed as the chief intelligence officer to establish spy networks in northern Russia. Michael Smith, the author of *Six: A History of Britain's Secret Intelligence Service,* wrote of Thornhill:

He was setting up agent networks across the north between Murmansk and the White Sea port of Kem to warn the British of any Bolshevik advances ... Thornhill was allocated as the force's chief intelligence officer, and a number of MI1c officers who worked with him.

Although not an agent like Paul Dukes or Sidney Reilly, he did a good job with his couriers. In 1939 he married Rachel Crowdy, the Chief of the Department of Opium Traffic and Social Issues Section for the League of Nations. He died in 1952.

### Ernest Boyce

Ernest Boyce was employed by the Russian mining industry before the First World War. As a Russian linguist, he was recruited by the SIS during the war and was sent out to Petrograd to join the small group of agents lead by Robert Bruce Lockhart. Boyce was described as a 'silver-haired lieutenant with considerable experience in military sabotage.' Sidney Reilly arrived in Russia and stayed long enough to meet Boyce, who was the new head of British MI6 in Petrograd. He took over after the departure of Major Stephen Alley and had been appointed to oversee intelligence operation against Germany.

During the attack on the Petrograd Embassy on 31 August, Boyce was one of the SIS agents rounded up and threatened with execution. Boyce and his colleagues were surprisingly released on 1 September and he was the only one aware of Reilly's planned coup, but even he did not know that it had been exposed by the Cheka. Boyce then went on to work as a Passport Control Officer in Tallinn, Estonia before being appointed SIS chief in Helsinki. Boris Savinkov, a left-wing member who hated the Bolsheviks, was a friend of Sidney Reilly, who wrote a letter that was published in *The Morning Post* on 8 September, 1924. He had crossed the border into Russia on 10 August and was promptly arrested, condemned to death and finally released. The letter was published in the *The Morning Post* but Reilly informed Boyce and dismissed it as written by the GPU.

I claim the great privilege of being one of his most intimate friends and devoted followers, and on me devolved the sacred duty of vindicating his honour. Contrary to the affirmation of your correspondent, I was one of the very few who knew his intention to penetrate into Soviet Russia. On receipt of a cable from him, I hurried back at the beginning of July, from New York, where I was assisting my friend, Sir Paul Dukes, to translate and to prepare for publication Savinkov's later book, The Black Horse ... Since my arrival here on July 19th, I have spent every day with Savinkov up to August 10th, the day of his departure for the Russian frontier.

Boris Savinkov died on 7 May, 1925. According to the Bolshevik government, he was arrested then committed suicide by jumping from a window in the Lubyanka Prison. Other sources say he was defenestrated, or killed in prison by members of the GPU. In 1925 – after a number of delays caused by Sidney Reilly's debt-ridden business dealings – Boyce sent Reilly across the Finnish border to his death, without clearing the scheme with London. Harry Carr, Boyce's assistant in Helsinki, stated: 'Boyce had to take some of the blame for the tragedy. Back in London he was carpeted by the Chief for the role he had played in this unfortunate affair.'

According to the Chekist, Alexander Orlov, he was convinced that the Allies were plotting against the Bolsheviks.

Lenin came to the conclusion that the British and French were definitely plotting to overthrow the Soviet government. He suggested to Dzerhinsky that it would be a good thing if the Cheka could catch the foreign plotters red-handed and expose them to the world.

In 1938 General Alexander Orlov, a senior figure in the Cheka (NKVD) defected to France, almost certainly because of the Great Purge. According to Orlov, 'Stalin decided to arrange for the assassination of Kirov and lay the crime at the door of the other former leaders of the opposition and thus with one blow do away with Lenin's former comrades.' Orlov later moved to the United States, where he was interviewed by Edward P. Gazur of the FBI, and he came out with the claim that Ernest Boyce was a double agent and was said to have information about British agents. He was said to be responsible for the betrayal of Sidney Reilly, which led to his execution. Nigel West (Rupert Allason) has argued that: 'The reason why this has not come out until now is that Orlov who was debriefed by British Intelligence, never told anybody but Edward Gazur.'

# Chapter Four

# The Newspaper Reporters

The public's interest during the First World War focused on the deaths and wounds of their loved ones and very few were interested in the events in Russia. British, French and American newspapers had sent journalists to cover what was happening in this huge land, but by 1917, the public were more interested in the Passchendaele battle than the machinations of a March Revolution and the Bolshevik's undermining of the aristocracy. In 1918–19 the reservations of President Woodrow Wilson did not stop the British sending munitions and clothing to Archangel in the hope that Russia would arm themselves and overwhelm the Bolsheviks. Over 300,000 Allied troops were sent to fight the Germans but remained to fight the Red Army. The Allies were made up of British, French, American and Italian soldiers. Elsewhere were Australian, New Zealander, Canadian and Japanese troops, as well as troops from almost every country in Europe. They hoped to beat the Red Army by surrounding Moscow and Petrograd and by using the economic blockade. Their actions increased Russian casualties due to famine, disease and civil war which reduced the population close to 14 million.

Most of the journalists failed to meet the challenge and – much like their editors – had little idea what Bolshevism was. One such journalist was New Zealander Harold Whitmore Williams. Writing for *The Times* and *Daily Chronicle*, he was an outstanding polyglot; he is said to have spoken over fifty-eight languages. He became foreign editor of *The Times*. While in Russia in the early years, he met Adriadna Tyrkova, who was arrested and sentenced to thirty months in prison. She fled to Stuttgart, where she met Williams and they moved to Paris together. They married in 1906 and moved to St Petersburg soon after. She later became a member of the Constitutional Democratic Party and briefly served as member of the Duma under Alexander Kerensky.

In 1916 Williams and Hugh Walpole were instructed by the Foreign Office to set up a British Propaganda Office in Petrograd. They cooperated with the Russian press and organised the bringing together of the Allies with an interchange of ideas between the Russian and the British. Throughout 1917 Williams sent regular dispatches to the *Daily Chronicle* up until March 1918, the date of the Brest-Litovsk Treaty. In February 1917 he wrote:

> All attention here is concentrated on the food question, which for the moment has become unintelligible. Long queues before the baker's shops have been a normal feature of life in the city. Grey bread is now sold instead of white, and cakes are not baked. Crowds wander about the streets, mostly women and boys, with a sprinkling of workman. Here there are windows broken and a few bakers shops looted. But, on the whole, the crowds are remarkably good-tempered and present cheer the troops, who are patrolling the streets.

Williams welcomed the overthrow of Tsar Nicholas and his family in March 1917:

> It is a wonderful thing to see the birth of freedom. With freedom comes brotherhood and in Petrograd today there is a flow of brotherly feeling. Everywhere you see it in the streets. The trams are not running. And people are tired of endless walking. But the habit now is to share your cab with perfect strangers. The police have gone, but the discipline is marvellous. Everyone shares the task of maintaining discipline and order. The volunteer militia has been formed and seven thousand men enrolled as special constables, mostly students, professors, and men of the professional classes generally. These, with the help of occasional small patrols of soldiers, control the traffic, guard the banks, factories, and Government buildings and ensure security.

With Kerensky in control, the summer of 1917 passed reasonably peacefully, but then come the Bolshevik Revolution in October, the mood declined. During the years from November 1917 to November 1919 the *New York Times* reported that the Bolsheviks were about to fall no fewer than ninety-one times. Williams despised the Bolsheviks; he was anti-semitic and filled his reports with defamatory comments about the party until he and his wife were forced to flee the city and they returned to London. While in London, he was recruited into the Committee on

Russian Affairs. He was one of the few people who knew the Russian leaders well, and he remembered Trotsky's final words to him before he left Russia, 'it will be the happiest day of my life when I see a revolution in England.'

One foreign correspondent who made his way to the Polish Front was Robert Liddell of *The Sphere* (an illustrated weekly). He arrived at the Polish Front and as a member of the Red Cross, he persuaded the Russian 165th Regiment to make him an honorary officer. The 165th Regiment had about 4,000 men but over 36,000 replacements passed through it in one year, something Liddell refused to pass on to *The Sphere*. The tactics of the White Russian officers were to send wave after wave of troops against the Germans in the hope that the sheer weight of numbers would break the enemy. Very little of the Russian Revolution found its way into the newspapers and – with the exception of Liddell – the Russian government refused to allow war reporters anywhere near the front. He later moved to Tiflis, Georgia and became a press censor with the Allied forces.

Robert Wilton had been in Russia from an early age and became conversant with the Russian language. His father was a mining engineer employed by Russia, and Wilton had a son who signed up with the Russian army in the First World War. He had joined the *New York Herald* in 1889 and stayed with the newspaper for fourteen years until he changed to *The Times*. During the fighting, Robert Wilton received the Cross of St George while serving with the Russians. As a serving officer, he sent reports and photographs back to London but he left out the terrible death rate of the Russian soldiers as he was loath to share the huge casualty toll with his weekly magazine. With such a large number of men in the army, he was aware that many of the Russian soldiers were sent to the trenches without proper clothing, boots or in many cases, rifles. Robert Wilton became special correspondent in Petrograd and Moscow. He was close to Moscow Station when he heard shots fired but by the time he reached the scene, the crowd had been dispersed and the snow was covered in blood. Wilton wrote:

> The fine weather brought everybody out of doors, and as the bridges and approaches to the great thoroughfare were for some unaccountable reason left open, crowds of all ages and conditions

made their way to the Nevsky, till the miles separating the Admiralty from the Moscow Station were black with people. Warnings not to assemble were disregarded. No Cossacks were visible. Platoons of Guardsmen were drawn up here and there in courtyards and side streets. The crowd was fairly good-humoured, cheering the soldiers, and showing themselves ugly only towards the few visible police.

Shortly after 3 pm orders were given to the infantry to clear the street. A company of Guards took up their station near the Sadovaya and fired several shots in the direction of the Anichkov Palace. Something like one hundred people were killed or wounded. On the scene of the shooting hundreds of empty cartridge cases were littered in the snow, which was plentifully sprinkled with blood.

After the volleys the thoroughfare was cleared but the crowd remained on the sidewalks. No animosity was shown towards the soldiers. The people shouted, 'We are sorry for you Pavlovsky (Guards Regiment). You had to do your duty.'

In some desperation, Wilton wrote to his foreign editor, Wickham Steed, 'Things are in an appalling state ... chaos had poisoned all the lower branches of the administrations ... I hear from all sides that there is a plot to get rid of the Emperor and Empress.' This information was ignored and instead Steed wrote in *The Times*, 'Russia Firm and United'. Wilton wrote about the murder of Rasputin in detail and received the following reply: 'The editor, influenced to some degree by a hint from the Foreign Office, decided that the details, though of lurid interest, were not fit for the columns of *The Times*.'

Morgan Philips Price, a journalist for the *Manchester Guardian*, took Wilton to task:

I have been appalled at the abominable behaviour of the Northcliffe Press in England, especially of its correspondent, Wilton, in Petrograd, whom, by the way, I know quite well, for spreading the provocative reports about the Union of Soldiers and Workers, and trying to discredit them in Western Europe. I only hope the Russian people will turn *The Times* correspondent out of Petrograd.

On 12 March 1917, *The Telegraph* office in Petrograd closed for three days and the British newspapers received no reports as to what was going on. The Foreign Office decided not to release any news until things became clearer. Wilton's office was beside the Prefecture where all the tsar's ministers had taken shelter, and he wrote:

> On a rough computation, four-fifths of the city is in the hands of the troops who have gone over to the Duma. Moreover, a huge number of the inhabitants are armed with rifles, revolvers and swords. There is still a good deal of casual firing, but on the whole the armed crowds behave well. They successively stormed and gutted all the police stations, carefully destroying all papers, and releasing prisoners.

*The Times* backed Wilton in his support of a democratic republic and wrote – with a caveat: 'A democratic republic in present conditions would inevitably result in disruption with wholesale bloodshed and ultimately, in reaction.'

With the March Revolution, Wilton visited the northern front. He left *The Times* and used a Reuters telegram to report Lenin's return to Russia. A workers demonstration in Petrograd in which they carried banners demanding that Lenin should return to the Kaiser. Wilton, age 52 at the time, was a right wing anti-semite who wrote that the Romanov family were killed as a ritual murder by the Jews. He was firmly anti-Jewish and became involved in the plot to get the tsar's family out of Russia. He was castigated by the Petrograd Society of Journalists who wrote an open letter to the Union of English Journalists complaining about Robert Wilton's bias in his reports. After the Revolution, he moved to Siberia following the collapse of Admiral Alexander Kolchak's government. He managed to escape from Russia and eventually arrived in Paris, where he rejoined the *New York Herald*.

The March Revolution saw large sections of the population release political prisoners. William J. Gibson, a resident of Petrograd, noted that 'Two men and a woman ... not old, all three were practically white-haired. They were political prisoners, and had been in close solitary confinement since 1905, the year of the first, defeated revolution.'

As summer turned into autumn, the population grew highly sceptical of the Provisional Government's inability to implement the economic and social resentment among the lower classes. General Levr Kornilov was appointed commander-in-chief of the Russian army in July 1917 and because of the Bolshevik's ability to gather a powerful army of workers and soldiers, they were able to counter Kornilov's coup as a dismal failure. The Provisional Government was distrusted among Russians and by October, the Bolsheviks had taken back control.

Arthur Ransome of the *Daily News* reported that the city was evolving in to pot of porridge, with bubbles breaking out here and there. The revolution had started. The following day demonstrators broke into the notorious Krestovsky Prison and released all the political prisoners, who then ran amok in the streets, smashing shop windows and attacking the police. One English eyewitness wrote that 'They were out for business and carried crowbars, hammers and lengths of weighted, tarred and knotted rope.'

Arthur Ransome wrote: 'Only those who know how things were but a week ago can understand the enthusiasm of us who have seen the miracle take place before our eyes. It is as if honesty had returned ... the day as one of rather precarious excitement, like a Bank Holiday with thunder in the air.'

A huge rally took part in Znamenskaya Square, centred on the statue of Alexander III, and few in the vast crowd could hear what the orators were saying. Finally, the crowds were dispersed and the police found the word 'Hippopotamus' engraved at the base of the statue for some reason.

Arthur Ransome was permitted to attend the Bolshevik's Executive Committee and the Third All-Russian Congress of Soviets.

> My position was immediately behind and above the presidium looking down on Trotsky's muscular shoulders and great head and the occasional gestures of his curiously small hands. Beyond him was a sea of men: soldiers in green and grey shirts, workers in collarless ones or jerseys, others dressed very much like a British workmen, peasants in belted red shirts and high top boots. My complete lack of any political past was a help not a hindrance and I was soon getting a view of what was happening from a much nearer than any regular journalist or politician could approach.

Ransome was a sometimes-spy for the British but still wrote about Bolsheviks. Alone among the Westerners in Petrograd, he was on intimate terms with the Bolshevik leaders. He saw them every day drinking their tea, hearing their quarrels, sharing with them such sweets as I had.' 'Meeting all these people as human beings, I could not believe the rubbishy propaganda that was being poured out by other Russians who, hoping for their destruction no matter by whom pretended that they were German agents.'

Unbeknown to anyone in London, Ransome had fallen in love with Trotsky's personal secretary, Yevgenia Shelepina. It was Yevgenia who typed up Trotsky's correspondence and planned all his meetings and suddenly Ransome found he had access to highly secretive documents and telegraphic transmissions. Over the autumn and winter of 1918, Ransome worked for the *Daily News* and through Yevgenia had access to Trotsky's intelligence. As Robert Bruce Lockhart observed to the Foreign Office in May 1919, Shelepina working with Ransome was instrumental in getting the numerous Boshevik papers and literature out of Russia. In December 1918 an agent told MI6 that Ransome, who was known as S76, had done quite good work. He was urged to leave the *Daily News* and return to Russia as a representative of the British Museum to collect all available documents with a bearing on Bolshevism. Ransome thought this would flatter the Bolsheviks and enable him to travel everywhere and collect everything to do with the communists.

Cumming put the plan to Willian Tyrrell, Head of the Political Intelligence Department of the Foreign Office on 19 December 1918, in which he stated;

> Ransome was probably the one person available to go openly to Moscow and Petrograd, and give us first hand information on the condition of things, and at any rate the ostensible policies that are being pursued there.

Tyrrell approved the scheme, and Ransome spent six weeks in Russia in February to March 1919, but there is no evidence that he was able to supply much useful intelligence during this period. Ransome's main concern was to get Yevgenia Shelepina out of Russia and into England. The opinion of one agent in the Stockholm office was that S76 was scrupulously honest.

> His reports about Russia could be relied upon absolutely with only the proviso that his view tends to be coloured by his personal sympathies with men like Litvinov and Radek (respectively the Soviet envoy in London and a member of the Bolshevik Central;

Executive Committee) ... He reports was he sees and does not see quite straight.

One of the most accomplished journalists who covered the period of the two revolutions was Morgan Philips Price, who was born in Gloucester in 1885. He studied science at Cambridge University and when he was 25, he joined a British expedition to explore the headwaters of the Enesei River in Central Siberia with two friends, Douglas Carruthers and J.H. Miller. He was against the war with Germany and his newspaper, the *Manchester Guardian*, asked him in 1914 to cover the events in Russia as he had mastered the language. Price had been recruited by the editor, C. P. Scott.

> He asked me to lunch at his house in Fallowfield and there we arranged something that was to become one of the turning points of my life. It turned out that Scott had been thinking just as I had. He scouted the whole idea that Tsarist Russia was going to change as a result of being allied to us and France; rather he feared the reverse might happen. He wanted someone to go to Russia for the *Manchester Guardian* and keep him informed about what was happening there. He might not be able to publish everything that was sent for reasons connected to the War, but at least he wanted to be informed.

Arriving in Petrograd, he reported the overthrow of Tsar Nicholas and his family. In July, Kerensky became the leader of the Provisional Government. Seen as a champion of the working class, Kerensky was unwilling to end the war and by October the Bolsheviks had taken control. Price's views on communism conflicted with Scott's, who was a liberal. Scott's views had become so different from Price's that he sent another journalist, named David Soskice, to Petrograd. Within a short time, Soskice became Alexander Kerensky's secretary.

It was a very bad time for those who rejected the Bolsheviks, and starvation swept the country. Price was stirred by Trotsky's oratory and he asked the Russian workers to 'Join the new revolutionary army forming in Petrograd, Moscow and Kharkov and go forth, not to kill our comrades of Central Europe and the allied countries, but to persuade us against the common enemy.'

He was one of the few journalists to witness the March Revolution and the spluttering Bolshevik one that followed in October 1917. During the latter revolution when food was at a premium, he lost 1.5st in three weeks. Starving, he felt very lucky during this upheaval to bite the bullet and write about the events that were happening around him. He explained in the *Manchester Guardian* on 19 November 1917:

> The Government of Kerensky fell before the Bolshevik insurgents because it had no supporters in the country. The bourgeois parties and the generals and the staff disliked it because it would not establish a military dictatorship. The Revolutionary Democracy lost faith in it because after eight months it had neither given land to the peasants' not established State control of industries, nor advanced the cause of the Russian peace programme. Instead it brought off the July advance without guarantee that the Allies had agreed to reconsider war aims. The Bolsheviks thus acquired great support all over the country. In my journey in the provinces in September and October I noticed that every local Soviet had been captured by them.

He even managed to meet with Lenin, and his reports contained his own feelings towards the Bolshevik cause. He tried to persuade the British government to intervene in the revolution but to no avail. Price interviewed Lenin and wrote:

> Lenin struck me as being a man who, in spite of revolutionary jargon that he used, was aware of the obstacles facing him and his party. There is no doubt that Lenin was the driving force behind the Bolshevik Party. He was the brains and the planner, but not the orator or the rabble-rouser. That function fell to Trotsky. I watched the latter, several times that evening, rouse the Congress delegates, who were becoming listless, probably through the long hours of excitement and waiting. He was always the man who could say the right thing at the right moment. I could see that there was the beginning now that fruitful partnership between him and Lenin that did so much to carry the Revolution through the critical periods that were coming.

In November 1918, the Germans signed the Treaty with the Allies. Price set off for Berlin, where he met Rosa Luxemburg, who had just been released from prison. He reported his meeting:

She asked me if the Soviets were working entirely satisfactorily. I replied, with some surprise, that of course they were. She looked at me for a moment, and I remember an indication of slight doubt on her face, but she said nothing more. Then we talked about something else and soon after I left. Though at the moment when she asked me that question I was taken aback. I soon forgot about it. I was still so dedicated to the Russian Revolution, which I had been defending against the Western Allies' war of intervention, that I had had no time for anything else.

Rosa Luxemburg had rallied the population to the socialist cause and, within a few days, she was arrested, clubbed to death and her body thrown into the River Spree. Price was warned about the anti-communist movement in Britain and left the *Manchester Guardian* to become the correspondent in Berlin for the *Daily Herald*. In July 1919 he was arrested for spreading Bolshevik propaganda and held for four days. On his release, he married Lisa Balster, who had been Luxemburg's secretary. Together they had two children but he faced hostility in Britain for having a German wife. In 1921 he returned to England with his family and in 1922 he quit journalism and ran as an MP. It took until 1935 but he got elected and he held the seat for the Forest of Dean until 1959.

The windows of the Winter Palace were shattered in October 1917. A cry went up proclaiming that the *duma* had surrendered. They had taken refuge in the Malachite Room, one of hundreds of rooms, and they waited for the revolutionaries to burst in and arrest them. All were arrested except for Kerensky, who managed to elude the Bolsheviks and escape from Russia. Radical journalist John Reed took part and he noticed that the corridors were packed with a crowd of unruly revolutionaries who grabbed anything that took their fancy. Someone called 'Comrades! Don't take anything. This is the property of the People!' In fact, John Reed, a dyed-in-the-wool communist, had grabbed a jewelled sword which he tucked inside his winter coat. His sympathies with the Bolshevik revolution did not stop him filching public property. He wrote in his best-selling book, *Ten Days That Shook the World*:

It was absolutely dark, and nothing moved but pickets of soldiers and Red Guards, grimly intent. In front of the Kazan Cathedral a three-inch field-gun lay in the middle of the street, slewed sideways from the recoil of its last shot over the roofs. Soldiers were standing in every doorway talking in loud tones and peering down towards the Police Bridge. I heard one voice saying: 'It is possible that we have done something wrong …' At the corners patrols stopped all passers-by – and the composition of these patrols was interesting, for in command of the regular troops was invariably a Red Guard … The shooting ceased …

We came out into the cold, nervous night murmurous with obscure armies on the move, electric with patrols. From across the river, where loomed the darker mass of Peter-Paul, came a hoarse shout … Underfoot the sidewalk was littered with broken stucco, from the corner of the Palace where two shells from the battleship Aurora had struck; that was the only damage done by the bombardment.

It was now after three in the morning. On the Nevsky all the street-lights were again shining, the cannon gone, and the only signs of war were the Red Guards and soldiers squatting around fires. The city was quiet – probably never so quiet in its history; on that night not a single hold-up occurred, not a single robbery.

In January, 200g rations of bread were distributed using ration cards and from the end of April, the daily allowance was reduced to 50g. Infectious diseases appeared in the city, and epidemics of typhus and abdominal typhoid began. The former health system continued to function. On-call doctors and pharmacies were working, and ambulances provided medical assistance, although often – due to a lack of petrol – ambulance cars could not set off even in cases where emergency assistance was needed.

On 3 March, 1918, the Brest-Litovsk Peace Treaty was signed by the Soviet regime in Russia. With the ensuing anarchy, the cancellation of state loans, the closure of banks and the absence of official quotations of stock prices, it was impossible to compile estimates of expenditure by organisations. Following the signing of the Brest-Litovsk Peace Treaty, chaos in Petrograd intensified and the city was gripped by panic. Famine broke out in Petrograd and this contributed to the government's move to Moscow on 11 March.

# Chapter Five

# Enter Paul Dukes

On 10 February 1889, Paul Henry Dukes was born as the third of five children in Bridgewater, Somerset. His father was the Reverend Edwin Joshua Dukes, a Congregationalist clergyman from London, and his mother was Edith Mary Pope from Somerset. Paul's mother was an exceptionally gifted woman who obtained her Bachelor of Arts degree by a correspondence course at the age of 20. In 1884 she married Edwin, who had returned from missionary work in China. In 1907 she died in her forties from a disease of the thyroid gland. The widowed Edwin married 40-year-old Harriet Rowse in 1909 and departed on an extended honeymoon.

Paul's siblings made their mark. Ashley Dukes was a playwright and Cuthbert became a renowned physician. The youngest brother, Marcus, died working as a government official in Kuala Lumpur. The exception was his elder sister, Irene Dukes, whose life was sadly cursed by illness. Paul was sent to a school in Caterham, the same school as Ashley, before boarding at Charterhouse School in Godalming, where he was encouraged to pursue his great gift in music. He was following in the illustrious footsteps of a former pupil, Ralph Vaughan Williams. He left school in 1907, two years before his father remarried. Deciding to leave the family, Dukes chose to travel to Petrograd to study music. With little money, Dukes arrived in the Netherlands and applied for a position as a music and English teacher in Rotterdam. He lasted a year with his teacher, William Birkett, before moving to Germany. He began working for Dr E. Kummer, before travelling to Warsaw, then part of the Russian Empire. He then moved onto Riga, the capital of Latvia, where he discovered Kummer was a deserter in the German army. He somehow managed to scrape a living in Riga, which took him to Petrograd in April 1910.

His two-year travels led him to enrol in the Conservatoire where he stayed for four years. He studied under renowned teacher Anna

Essipova, who had trained Sergie Prokofiev and Alexandra Borobsky, and he shared rooms with Sydney Gibbes, the tutor to the tsar's only son, Alexis. Graduating from the Conservatoire in August 1913, Dukes came to the attention of Russian-born English conductor Albert Coates, who offered to take him on as an assistant at the Marinsky Theatre, the home of the Imperial Opera and Ballet Company. He not only became word-perfect in Russian but he also coached opera singers, copied music and taught piano. When war was declared in 1914, he went to the British Embassy and entered his name as a volunteer for active service. Albert Coates promised to keep a place for Dukes at the Marinsky Theatre when he returned.

However, at his medical examination it was found that his heart was not sound enough for him to enlist, so instead of returning to Britain, the Foreign Office took advantage of Dukes' fluency in Russian to appoint him to the Anglo-Russian Commission in 1915. This was an offshoot of the British Department of Information which was established in Petrograd and was involved in arranging propaganda and supplies to Russia. His chief was John Buchan, the celebrated author, who agreed that Dukes should have a roving commission to travel about Russia picking up the views and opinions from the population as to how the war was progressing. Dukes' duty was to supply a daily précis that appeared in the press and the views of Russian citizens to the British ambassador, Sir George Buchanan, and the Foreign Office in London. When the revolution broke out in March 1917, Dukes enthusiastically embraced it, for he had no love for the old Tsarist system. With the outbreak of the Bolshevik Revolution in October, the Anglo-Russian Commission was wound up and returned to London.

At this time, Dukes had become very friendly with *Daily Chronicle* journalist Arthur Ransome, who had been taken ill and swapped newspapers. Standing in for his sick friend, Dukes had undertaken Ransome's work as special correspondent and wrote about Lenin even before his arrival in Petrograd. Some of Dukes' colleagues ridiculed Lenin having any significance, but Leon Trotsky and Gregory Zinoviev, whose real names were Bronstein and Apfelbaum, urged the masses to overturn the Tsarist regime. Both Dukes and Ransome were on hand to witness the first Kerensky Russian Revolution in March 1917.

In July 1917 Dukes was recalled to the Foreign Office, where he worked as a civil servant, so he missed the October Bolshevik seizure of the Provisional Government. Later he visited the Western Front, where he studied the work of various auxiliary organizations serving the soldiers, and reported whether they could serve on the Russian front. The Russian front was dissolving rapidly, and when he returned to London in November, he found out that the Bolsheviks were now in control and Kerensky had escaped across the frontier. Dukes applied to John Buchan, and asked for more active duties. He was sent to the front again, and witnessed things that had a profound effect on him, like the shootings and the bombardment as the troops attacked the German lines. In December 1917 he made the trip back into Russia, using a King's Messenger passport and a dozen diplomatic bags to deliver to the British embassies in Oslo, Stockholm and Petrograd.

He found Russia in a thoroughly depressing state. Lenin had arrived at the Finland Station from Germany and delivered a speech to the few of his supporters. Among those who heard his words was Paul Dukes. Lenin had decreed that everything had to be shared but it did not work that way. Buying and selling was regarded a crime, while houses and furniture was proclaimed common property to be administered by the Communist Party. Transport had broken down and cities were without food or fuel. 'House Committees' consisting of illiterate beggars, tramps and peasants issued 'certificates of identification' and 'sojourn permits' and had no compunction in turning the inhabitants out into the streets. These middle-class people were quickly dubbed *kulaks* or 'grabbers' who stole goods by the 'Committees'. In 1921, Lenin announced that his terrible experiment was a failure and he ordered a reversal of policy that led to 'construction instead of destruction.'

Dukes then attached himself to the American YMCA in the eastern town of Samara, where he held parades and organised sporting events for the scouts, much to the bewilderment of the Bolsheviks. In June 1918 he received a message from the consul general asking him to return to Moscow immediately. When he arrived, he was handed a telegram from the Foreign Office ordering him to return to London. He caught a train to Petrograd (Moscow was now the capital of Russia) and then another train to Archangel. He travelled by steamer to Murmansk, where he caught a destroyer which took him to Petchenga, 135 miles west of Murmansk.

He transferred to a tug, which took him around the North Cape. His broken journey had taken him to Norway where he found a place on the troopship *Prince Arthur,* which docked in Aberdeen on 26 July 1918.

At King's Cross, a car was waiting to take him to Whitehall and in one of the turnings on the left – Whitehall Mansions – he found Mansfield Cumming and his staff. An elevator took him to the top floor, and following his guide he was led through a rabbit warren of corridors, stairs and offices and crossed an iron bridge until he reached a small office. Here he was met by the deputy head, Colonel Freddy Browning, father of Arnhem commander 'Boy' Browning. He was greeted with the words:

> You doubtless wonder that no explanation has been given to you as to why you should return to England. Well, I have to inform you, confidentially, that it has been proposed to offer you a somewhat responsible post in the Secret Intelligence Service. We have reason to believe that Russia will no longer continue to be open to foreigners. We wish someone to remain there to keep us informed of the march of events.

Dukes and Browning did not hit it off; the latter was urging him to enrol but Dukes had no intention of working for the Intelligence Service. He was introduced to Sir Robert Nathan, the head of MI6's political intelligence department, Section V, who expounded his views on Russia. He left Dukes alone in his office, saying he was going to see if Cumming was ready to receive his new recruit. Dukes was drawn to the bookshelf and spotted the works by William Makepeace Thackeray. He picked up one of Thackeray's novels:

> When I took down *Henry Esmond* it turned out to be a dummy. There was nothing to distinguish it outwardly from its fellows. I was about to put it back quickly when, my finger accidentally touching a catch-spring, the cover opened and a few sheets of paper fell out. As I hastily gathered them up I noticed the heading Kriegsministerium Berlin, and minute handwriting in German … Barely had I replaced the volume when the head of the department returned.

Cumming was not available and the next day Dukes was once again in the same room with Nathan, who wished to initiate him into the secrets of the department. Dukes rose and took down *Henry Esmond,* expecting to find it was a dummy. 'To my utter confusion it opened quite naturally and I found in my hands nothing more than an edition de luxe of *Henry Esmond*.' His guide had replaced the volume, and without comment, took Dukes to see Cumming. In his book, *Red Dusk and the Morrow*, Dukes related his first meeting with 'C':

> It was a low, dark chamber at the extreme top of the building. The colonel knocked, entered, and stood at attention. Nervous and confused, I followed, painfully conscious that at that moment I could not expressed a sane opinion on any subject under the sun. From the threshold the room seemed bathed in semi-obscurity. The writing desk was so placed with the window behind it that on entering everything appeared in silhouette. It was some seconds before I could clearly distinguish things. A row of half-a-dozen extending telephones stood at the left of a big desk littered with papers. On a side table were numerous maps and drawings, with models of aeroplanes, submarines, and mechanical devices, while a row of bottles of various colours and a distilling outfit with a rack of test tubes bore witness to chemical experiments and operations. These evidences of scientific investigation only served to intensify an already overpowering atmosphere of strangeness and mystery.

It was some eighteen months later that Dukes was able to give a description of Cumming:

> This extraordinary man was short of stature, thick-set with grey hair covering a well-rounded head. His mouth was stern and an eagle eye, full of vivacity, glanced, or glared as the case maybe, piercingly through a gold-rimmed monocle. At first encounter, he appeared very severe and his manner of speech abrupt. Yet the stern countenance could melt into the kindliest of smiles, and the softened eyes and lips revealed a heart that was big and generous.

Finishing a page he was reading, Cumming looked up and said, 'I understand you want to go back to Soviet Russia, do you?' He was joined by Lieutenant Colonel Lort Rhys Samson, who had been the Athens head of station and they spoke together for a short time before Cumming ended the conversation. Cumming's idea was for Dukes to overhaul the shattered intelligence structure inside Russia thanks to a British businessman who would give him his agents and couriers. He would be alone and it would be down to him to rebuild the network of couriers to smuggle out his reports. Cumming told him: 'We have reason to believe that Russia will not long be open to foreigners. We want someone to remain there to keep us informed of the march of events … Don't go and get killed.'

During the winter months when ice and snow limited speed, this was a rather slow-moving process, and it was left to Mansfield Cumming to speed it up. Dukes was then given a three-week crash course in ciphers and invisible inks before being sent off to Petrograd. Dukes was ordered not to conspire after returning to Russia, but to inquire; he was also instructed in a vague way to survive and find his own way out of Russia.

> As to the means whereby you gain access to the country, under what cover you will live there and how you will send your reports, we shall leave it to you, being best informed as to conditions, to make suggestions.

Two weeks later, Dukes received instructions to visit an office in the Strand. Here he was handed a note which read 'Kingston station midnight Sunday'. He arrived shortly before midnight but had to wait until 3.00 am, watching the trains carrying solders to their camps. At last he was met by a messenger who told him to get out at Newcastle. The journey was circuitous; it took him to Bristol, Birmingham and finally Newcastle in the evening. Another messenger met him and took him to a troop ship, *Olympia*, which carried a detachment of US Marines bound for Archangel.

Arriving at the White Sea port, he met two agents from Military and Naval Intelligence, Colonel Cudbert Thornhill and Lieutenant Commander Malcolm MacLaren, who advised him not to travel from Archangel to Petrograd but to go to Finland and cross the border closer to Petrograd. Dukes had intended walking to Petrograd, but spotting a snowstorm, said:

> You've won. I'll go to Finland. I dare say that I owe my life to Thornhill for holding me back from an attempt to cross those limitless wastes on foot in bad weather. He fitted me out with a passport of a Norwegian travelling salesman … I made my way through Norway

to Stockholm. Here I became 'Sergei Ilitch', a Serbian, travelling for business to Helsingfors.

Arriving at the start of winter, Dukes took Thornhill's advice and crossed the border into Finland. He arrived in Helsingfors (Helsinki), a city that was a dumping ground for every kind of rumour, slander or scandal, especially from the Germans and Russians. Dukes was introduced to an agent of the American Secret Service, who handed Dukes a letter to give to a Russian named Melnikov in Viborg, near the border. Dukes, disguised as Sergei Ilitch, a commercial traveller, was booked into a small hotel in Viborg. He found that Melnikov was staying in the same hotel and that he had worked with Captain Francis Cromie. He also found that Melnikov had two places they could meet in Petrograd; the hospital and a small private café in an apartment. Dukes described his new companion:

Melnikov was slim, dark, with stubbly hair, blue eyes, short and muscular. He was deeply religious and imbued with an intense hatred of the Bolsheviks – not without reason, since both his father and his mother had been brutally shot by them, and he himself had only escaped by a miracle.

Dukes learned that Melnikov had managed to escape with his life, having witnessed his father being shot. His mother was executed a few weeks later.

I had some papers referring to an insurrection which my mother kept for me. My father barred the way, saying she was dressing. A sailor tried to push past, and my father angrily struck him aside. Suddenly a shot rang out, and my father fell dead on the threshold. I was in the kitchen when the Reds came, and through the door I fired and killed two of them. A volley of shots was directed at me. I was wounded in the hand and only just escaped by the back stairway. My mother was seized before I could get in again, and two weeks later she was executed on account of the discovery of my papers.

Melnikov was keen to return to Petrograd and wreak vengeance on the men who killed his parents. On 24 November he gave Dukes a slip of paper with a written password to hand to the Finnish border guards. He also informed Dukes of an English expatriate, an electrical engineer named John Merrett, also named Marsh, who was waiting for his imprisoned wife to escape and would hand over the entire spy network. Dukes had several bottles of Johnnie Walker whiskey, which Melnikov managed to get through. It was pretty obvious that his Russian friend was an alcoholic and had downed several bottles, but by 22 November 1918, Dukes managed to keep one bottle out of Melnikov's reach. He later wrote:

> At six o'clock he went into his room, returning in a few minutes so transformed that I hardly recognised him. He wore a sort of seaman's cap that came right down over his eyes. He had dirtied his face, and this, added to the three-days-old stubble on his chin, gave him a truly demoniacal appearance. He wore a shabby coat and trousers of a dark colour, and a muffler was tied closely round his neck. He looked a perfect apache as he stowed away a big Colt revolver inside his trousers.
>
> 'Good-bye' said Melnikov again. He turned, crossed himself, and passed out of the room. On the threshold he looked back. 'Sunday evening,' he added, 'without fail.' I had a curious feeling I ought to say something, I knew not what, but no words came. I followed him quickly down the stairs. He did not look round again. At the street corner he glanced rapidly in every direction, pulled his cap still further over his eyes, and passed away into the darkness.

An associate of Melnikov – referred to as Ivan Sergeivich – gave Dukes some valuable information as he departed. It was a refuge he could use, being a run-down apartment in Petrograd still occupied by his housekeeper. Dukes visited the Viborg market place and bought a Russian shirt, black leather breeches, black knee boots and an old cap, which allowed his shaggy hair to dangle in front of his eyes. Catching a train to Raiaioki about half a mile from the frontier, he met up with a group of Finnish border guards, who were briefed to know how to prepare certificates of identification. Dukes was given a Ukrainian name, Joseph Ilitch Afirenko, and one of the Finns – to Dukes' surprise – furnished Dukes with a Certificate of Service in the Cheka! (Tchrezvichaika – the Extraordinary Commission)

> This is to certify that Joseph Afirenko is in the service of the Extraordinary Commissar of the Central Executive Committee of the Petrograd Soviet of Workers and Red Army men's Deputies in the capacity of office clerk, as the accompanying signatures and seals attest.

Handing over a portrait photograph, it was glued to the side of the certificate and stamped by two five-pointed stars with a hammer and a plough in the centre. Taking a round rubber seal, two imprints were made on the photograph. Another paper was quickly printed with the words: 'The holder of this is the Soviet employee, Joseph Ilitch Afirenko, aged 36.' The leader of the guards produced a box full of rubber stamps.

> Soviet seals. We keep ourselves up to date. Some of them are stolen; some we made ourselves and this one we bought from over the river for a bottle of vodka.

The wooden bridge that crossed the River Sestro at Raiaioki had a guard post which separated the two countries. Instead, Dukes was taken a couple of miles further north and away from the border crossing. Arriving at a ramshackle house by the river, Dukes waited until 3.00 am before moving. The Finns had hidden a small boat with ropes attached, and as Dukes reached the Russian side, he crashed through a sheet of ice by the far bank, plunging him into freezing water and soaking his legs and feet. This induced a painful frost bite which plagued him for many weeks. The crack of the ice disturbed the Red border guards, who began firing wildly into the night. He had been told to keep to the meadow and not the forest on either side. He was given a white sheet to cover himself on the meadow and luckily he managed to cross half-way on the sloping meadow on the Russian side and lay motionless until the shouting and gun-shots fell silent. Having missed the correct direction, he had to cross a small stream which added to his previous soaking. Managing to slip into a lane, he found a half-built house and sheltered there until dawn broke. He then marched down the road which led to a village station. Here, he caught a train that took over two hours and arrived at the Finland Station. It dawned on Dukes that he was the only British spy in Soviet Russia and he later wrote about how Petrograd looked:

> There was plenty of life and movement in the streets, though only foot-passengers. The roadway was dirty and strewn with litter. Strung across the street from house to house were the shreds of washed-out red flags, with inscriptions that showed they had been hung out to celebrate the anniversary of the Bolshevist coup d'état a few weeks earlier. Occasionally one came across small groups of people, evidently of the educated class, ladies and elderly gentlemen

in worn out cloths, shovelling away the early snow and slush under the supervision of a workman who, as taskmaster, stood still and did nothing.

Chaos and desolation, hatred, misery, suffering, disease and death – these were the first fruits of a communistic system. All around was shabbiness. Here and there lay a dead horse. The wretched brutes were whipped to get the last spark of life and labour out of them and they lay where they fell. For the ladies, who were made to sweep the streets, were not strong enough to remove dead horses.

He found that the cafés were all closed but odd apartments were used to sell tea and poor scraps of food. These were often raided by the Cheka, who closed the makeshift cafés and accused the proprietors of 'speculation.' He then set about looking for Melnikov. He frequented one of the cafés, which was on the top floor of a house in one of the roads that led off from the Nevsky Prospect. Here Dukes met Vera Alexandrovna, a pretty 20-year-old girl, and she seated Dukes in an empty room. Serving tea and delicious little cakes, something he would never have found in the city, Dukes asked Vera how she managed to keep the café going.

Oh, it is becoming very difficult indeed. We have two servants whom we send twice a week into the villages to bring back flour and milk, and we buy sugar from the Jews in the Jewish market. But it is getting so hard. We do not know if we shall be able to keep it going much longer. Then, too, we may be discovered. Twice the Reds have been to ask if suspicious people live in this house but the porter put them off because we gave him flour.

Dukes, posing as a shabbily dressed Russian, felt he stood out amongst the rest of the clientele as they came in. Unable to contact Melnikov, he was approached by one of the men sitting at a nearby table.

He was tall and thin, with shrunken eyes, hair brushed straight up, and a black moustache. There was a curious crooked twitch about his mouth. 'Good Afternoon,' he said, 'Allow me to introduce myself. Captain Zorinsky. You are waiting for Melnikov, are you not? I am a friend of his...' I resolved I would not stay in this café any longer. The atmosphere of the place filled me with indefinable apprehension.

Dukes had an aversion to Zorinsky, who had a shifty appearance, but later produced some good intelligence. He managed to find the apartment owned by Ivan Sergeievich and Melnikov, where he was able to stay for a couple of days. The apartment block was in darkness and Dukes had to bang on the door several times before he heard some conversation in the hallway. Eventually the door was opened and the housekeeper was in some nervous state as she had narrowly avoided being arrested that morning by the Cheka in the local marketplace. The flat was run by Melnikov's middle-aged housekeeper, named Stepanovna, accompanied by a young female nurse named Varia, who looked after Ivan Sergeivich's childen. They were fed on Red Army rations by the housekeeper's nephew, Dmitri, who was a soldier and was happy to feed the two women. Dukes asked Stepanovna if there was a Committee of the Poor in the house to which she replied that there was a committee made up of three servant girls, the yard keeper and the house porter. They administered the forty apartments but took any furniture they liked to furnish their apartments on the ground floor. (So much for the Committee of the Poor.)

Dukes had been instructed by Cumming to supply low-level intelligence on conditions in Russia. The catastrophic decline in living standards became apparent as soon as he entered Petrograd. The streets were filled with garbage, dead horses gave off a smell of decay and he saw lines of wretched people standing frozen in the arctic weather, offering their personal belongings in exchange for food. He saw the grand palaces that lined the Moika that had been taken over by the Bolsheviks. The head of the Cheka, Felix Dzerzhinsky, urged his officers to devote all their energies to a ruthless class war and called for 'the extermination of the enemies of the revolution on the basis of their class affiliation or their pre-revolutionary roles.' Dukes ventured out and described the change in Petrograd:

> The morning was raw and snow began to fall. People hurried along the streets huddling bundles and small parcels. Queues, mostly working women, were waiting outside small stores with notices printed on canvas over a lintel 'First Communal Booth', 'Second Communal Booth' and so on, where bread was being distributed in small quantities against food cards. There was barely enough to go round, so people came and stood early, shivering in the biting wind.

Similar queues formed later in the day outside larger establishments marked 'Communal Eating House, Number so-and-so' ... They received their modicum of bread, they would carry it hastily away, either in their bare hands, or wrapped up in paper bought for the purpose, or shielded under their shawls which they muffled around their ears and neck.

The market places of Petrograd are crowded daily with thousands selling every imaginable sort of goods; people with a few herrings in filthy pieces of newspaper, a number of individuals displaying on their open palms lumps of sugar at 6 or 7 roubles per lump.

The second night at Melnikov's apartment, Dukes was awakened by loud thumping on the door. Dressing quickly, he was confronted by the figure of Melnikov and behind him was a huge man, who was introduced as John Merrett. He was an Englishman, who had organised the courier service from the British spy networks for a few months but was now on the run. He worked for BECOS Traders – the British Engineering Company of Siberia – and he had begun installing the electricity in Petrograd. Merrett was part of the expatriate group who lived and worked in Petrograd, and as things became progressively fraught, Merrett managed to ferry some 250 fellow Britons by crossing the Finnish border some 30 miles north of Terrioki. He owned a farm to the east of Petrograd, and – despite the Cheka ransacking the buildings – was still able to obtain potatoes and flour. Although a businessman acting as an agent, he had been in contact with Francis Cromie and some of the other officers.

His second wife, Lydia Merrett, had been brought up in Russia. Although she had little to do with Merrett's activities, she was arrested as a hostage, taken to 2 Gorokhovaya Street and imprisoned in the Cheka's headquarters; a large, grey building built around a large courtyard with an archway that enabled the Chekist lorries to come and go. The courtyard was also used for executions that were timed at 7.00 pm. Merrett told Dukes how the secret police had tailed him for many weeks and just a few days earlier he had managed to escape as the Cheka burst into his flat. He rushed into the kitchen, opened the window and slithered down the drainpipe. He told Dukes of another escape, in which he was held under a lamppost by a Cheka agent. Screwing up his face into a grimace he asked for a light and as the agent hesitated, he knocked him down and ran away.

Paul Dukes was later interviewed by *The New York Tribune* on March 1921, and spoke of the freeing of Mrs Merrett from the Chekist.

Later I discovered that there had been raid on March's (Merrett) house shortly before the arrival that Mrs March, his wife, was arrested, but that he had escaped by running out the back door and jumping over the fence ... On the third day of my stay at the house a sheet of paper was slipped under the door, addressed to Paviol (?) Pavlovich, my Russian Christian name and patronymic. The note said 'You can meet March after dinner between 5 and 6 pm on the third bench from the iron gate in the Summer Garden, He will be blowing his nose continually with a red handkerchief. You can meet me at the Fifth Soviet eating house on the Nevsky.' The note was signed by Melnikoff, the pseudonym of the first officer who preceded me.

I met March and he told me the story of his escape. He said his wife was arrested that he was being dogged by agents of the Extraordinary Commission, and it was essential that he flee cross the frontier. I made this my first object to obtain the release of Mrs March. I did this with the aid of a former secret service official of the Cheka to whom I was introduced by March and who had also been in the service of Captain Cromie and now was a school inspector under the Bolsheviks. I will refer to him a Romanoff (the Policeman). An initial payment of 10,000 roubles sufficed to prepare the way for bribing the petty officers of the Extraordinary Commission guards, sentries etc ...

The place of detention was the famous, or infamous, 2 Gorochovaya, formally the city prefecture and now the place of the Bolshevik inquisition on St Petersburg and house of preliminary incarceration ... The place has since the advent of the Bolsheviki acquired the reputation of a house of blood and tears. Some day, when the story of 2, Gorochovaya is written it will eclipse the most gruesome tales of the torture chambers of the Middle Ages. All prisoners, especially Mrs March, were subjected to daily interrogation ... The final interrogation lasted from 10 o'clock until 6 o'clock in the evening without interruption until she swooned and fell in a faint. In the evening she was informed that she probably would be executed.

Meanwhile, Dukes had attended a communist meeting, which he found irksome. Leaving the meeting, he went to where people declared their interesting communist opinions instead. The main speakers were Trotsky and Zinoviev, who expressed themselves well and Dukes later wrote. 'The unrivalled powers of speech of a few of the leading Bolsheviks, who possess in a marked degree the fatal gift of eloquence, had an almost irresistible attraction.'

Dukes moved into a flat on Liteyny Prospekt owned by Kurz-Gedroitz, better known as Dmitri Konstantinovich, and known as 'the Journalist'. The flat was on the shady side of the street and was gloomy and icy cold. Konstantinovich was a thin man of 35 but looked more like 50. He constantly groaned about his problems but when Merrett gave him gritty black bread, he became all smiles. He had worked as a journalist but was forced to take the post of a clerk at the Department of Public Works and was able to get an official ration on which to live.

Merrett handed over all his underground contacts and agents to Dukes, including several who worked at the Ministry of War and the Admiralty. Merrett talked of his adventures and his farm on the outskirts of Petrograd, which had been pillaged by the Bolsheviks. He had known Cromie well and mentioned some names of people that Dukes might want to re-enlist. He also gave the addresses of the safe houses in the city. John Merrett told Dukes to follow him at a distance past the Cathedral, through the market place and into a labyrinth of streets until they reached Apartment No. 5.

After spending twenty-four hours at Apartment No. 5, Dukes completed his report made out on tracing paper and written in tiny writing. Dukes gave the tissue paper to Merrett, or Morometz as he was known, who hid it in his boot. They each caught a sleigh to Okhta Station, a rather crude edifice on the eastern side of the River Neva. On the wooden platform were hundreds of people waiting to board the train. Dukes managed to spot the hulking Merrett ahead and was able to describe his appearance.

> With his face smudged with dirt and decorated with three day's growth of reddish beard, a driver's cap that covered his ears and a big sack on his back, Murometz (Merrett) looked – well, like nothing on earth.

Waiting until he had clambered aboard an already overcrowded carriage, the hulking Merrett managed to make space for himself. The train slowly moved north and reached Grusino, and Merrett met up with his fellow escapee and together they avoided the Red Guards, who entered the carriages from the platform side. They both made their escape by leaving the train on the other side and disappeared into the woods. Eventually they found their guide's cabin and Merrett and his companion were then taken by sleigh to the border, about 30 miles away. Another guide was to take them across the frontier but he wanted to travel to Petrograd to sell his supply of matches that he had smuggled from Finland. Merrett came up with a solution. He bought the matches and made a present of them to his guide. The guide said he had been spotted sneaking across the border and he would take them to a vast snow-covered clearing and pointed to where the frontier was. Merrett and his companion sat in the shade of the trees not daring to move into the clearing.

> It was a nasty moment for my companion's nerves were already in shreds as a result of his former ill-luck. He began to think himself doomed to failure. But fortunately a blizzard came on and we were able to move forward under cover of the driving snow. It was hard going, but we trudged on in the teeth of the blizzard like the pictures of Polar explorers. At last we came to the dyke that marked the frontier, crossed it on a rickety plank, and that was the last we saw of the 'proletarian paradise'.

Dukes brought up the subject of the small, fat man as a private eye, who he knew as a former Tsarist secret policeman, named Alexei Fromvich.

> This man (the Policeman) was, I believe, an official of the okrana before the revolution, and is doing some sort of clerical work in a Soviet institution now. The Bolsheviks are re-engaging Tsarist police agents for the Extraordinary Commission (Cheka) so he had close connections there and knows most of what goes on. He is a liar and it is difficult to believe what he says, but, if you outbid the Bolsheviks, this fellow can do things, understand?

While alone with Alexei Fromvich, he received a frosty response. He was later told that he worked for the tsar as a policeman who sorted out problems among the many aristocrats who gravitated around the tsar's family. Dukes realised he had made a mistake and quickly changed the subject. The Policeman was a boastful individual who was short, red-faced and pompous but Dukes was anxious to obtain Mrs Merret's freedom by paying him handsomely to release her from prison. The Cheka had arrested several of Merrett's employees, including his wife, Lydia Merrett, and she was quickly sent to Chamber No. 4 at No. 2 Gorokhovaya Street (Pea Street). Held for nearly a month with thirty-eight other women – some high-class ladies, others prostitutes – in a cell that was too small to accommodate so many women. At 4 o'clock, starved, unable to wash and having to use a bucket as a toilet, her cell door was opened and her name was called. The Policeman was able to put in motion the means to spring her from captivity.

Full of dread, she followed the prison guard along the corridor, fully expecting to be led to an execution. Instead, they turned down a side passage which led to a ladies' toilet and the guard indicated that she should enter. In the corner lay a green shawl and a shabby hat, with two slips of paper attached. One of them was a pass in an unknown name, stating that she had entered the building at 4 o'clock and must leave at 7. The other just said, *'Walk straight into St Izaacs Cathedral'*, which she destroyed immediately. Dressed in the shawl and battered hat, she climbed the stairs to the ground floor, where the guard on the door barely glanced at the pass. Shuffling through the courtyard, she moved though the archway to the main gate, where another guard barely registered her proffered pass which he added to the rest of the paperwork. She slipped away; the feeling of freedom with no one following her was a novel experience, and soon she reached the Cathedral. Entering the little wooden side entrance, she was spotted by Paul Dukes, who had been waiting for her. Quietly, he spoke to Lydia Merrett saying that he was to accompany her into Finland.

Leaving the Cathedral, they crossed the square and took a cab to a place called Five Corners. Walking a few hundred yards, they caught another taxi and drove near Zorinsky Prospect and onto Merrett's No. 5 Apartment. Seeing that no Cheka was around, they climbed to the apartment and were greeted by Maria, who had become Dukes' mistress. Using a different name, Nadezhda Ivanovna Petrovskaya, she was in charge of the networks. She was a doctor and former revolutionary, but used the cover name Mariya Smirnova, and was referred to as Merrett's housekeeper. She was able to furnish productive intelligence to Dukes, but with gathering suspicion falling on her, she left Petrograd and hid in John Merrett's farm in the countryside. Surfacing again, Mariya continued keeping the network alive for a few months before she was arrested and sentenced to death. Languishing in prison, she was finally released in 1922.

On 18 December, Mariya and Dukes left No. 5 and made their way in the wind-blown snow which flung itself at the half-hidden faces that hurried along. Towards midday the storm abated as they entered the neighbouring market place to buy a cloak for Mrs Merrett. The corner of the Kuznetchny Pereulok and the Vladimirovsky Prospect was a busy place for the 'speculators', as private trading was prohibited. Many of the citizens were educated women who were selling off their last possessions in order to purchase food for their families. Old clothing, crockery, toys, knick-knacks, clocks, books, pictures, paper, pans and old jewellery were for sale. In addition, sugar, herrings and bread patties were also on sale. Mariya made for the clothing and found a warm but well-used cloak. Dukes did not bargain for it and surprisingly paid what the woman asked for it.

After an hour's rest, Lydia Merrett was dressed in the well-worn cloak with a black shawl, and departed. Dukes caught a sleigh and with Lydia barely able to move, they made their way to Okhta Station. As before, the platform was crowded and Dukes picked up the starving Lydia and found a spot in an extra box car. The crowd were crammed into the point of suffocation but after the screams and oaths, the train left in silence. After five hours of discomfort, they reached Grusino at midnight. Merrett had instructed Dukes to walk the other direction, cross the rails and take a path which led to a hut owned by a Finnish family. In the hut they found a small party gathering, which included two teenage girls, a French nursemaid and an officer who looked after them. A 16-year-old Finn named Fita had two sleighs ready to leave at 1.00 am. Dukes paid him extra, in case they had to make a run for it. The area around the border passes west of Lake Ladoga in terrain that freezes and is easily negotiated in winter. They travelled north and then west to a remote hut about 5 miles from the border. The party said their goodbyes to Fita, unaware that he had been tracked down and would be killed by the Cheka for 'conspiring with counter-revolutionaries'. Fita left them with a Finnish peasant who was to guide them on foot through the woods to the first Finnish village 10 miles away.

It was not until they were about to cross the frontier that Dukes realised that the two girls were daughters of the Grand Duke Paul Alexandrovich and the French nursemaid was Miss Herschelman. Dukes was amazed at the resilience of Lydia Merrett, who had suffered in prison for many weeks and with the prospect of being executed. She bore up well, better than the other ladies. Battling their way through the thick snow and ice, they reached a small stream. Their guide suddenly vanished into an invisible dyke but scrambled up on the other side having plunged through thin ice. Although the stream was narrow and the ice not thick enough, Dukes came up with an idea.

> If I threw myself across I might make a bridge with my body for the others to step over. Planting my feet firmly, I threw myself across the dyke, digging my hands into the other bank. I called to Mrs M, who was the pluckiest, to step on to my back and run across. She did so, and was followed by the other lady. Then came the two girls and finally Herschelman. When they were all safely over I wriggled across on my stomach.

They stumbled on until they reached the stream which was about 10ft wide. They made their way cautiously along the bank and suddenly came across a black figure who turned out to be an acquaintance of their guide. They were told of a rickety bridge at the end of the clearing. It turned out to be a thin, heavily iced plank which led to their promised land. They all managed to cross the slippery plank and they all crossed the border into Finland. Once over, the two girls fell on their knees and crossed themselves before sitting on a fallen tree trunk to eat their sandwiches. They all reached the Terrioki railway station without incident and took the train to Helsingfors. Mrs Merrett had suffered the interrogations, the threat of execution in the Cheka prison, the rigors of the freezing temperatures and was seen to be ill. She was kept at Terrioki and after a few weeks' recuperation she recovered and made her way to Helsingfors, where she met up with her husband, John Merrett. Together they returned to England and lived out their lives in East Sussex. Some years later, Dukes met up with John Merrett and his wife in his manor house, and they swapped tales of their escapades in Russia. John Merrett died in 1966, about the same time as Gus Agar and Paul Dukes.

Another part of Merrett's story included his estranged wife, Bertha, who could not stand the Petrograd climate, divorced him and in 1913, left for Switzerland. She was given custody of their son, 17-year-old,

John Donald, who grew up to be a sociopathic monster involved in fraud and racketeering. In 1924 Bertha took John to Britain to complete his education in the hopes that he would enter the diplomatic service. When this failed, she took him to Edinburgh College and rented a flat nearby. John stole a chequebook and drained his mother's account. In 1926, John shot and killed his mother, claiming she had committed suicide. He managed to escape the hangman with his plausible explanation about his mother's state of depression. Over the years, he was imprisoned several times for drug dealing, gunrunning and many similar sordid crimes. Desperate to continue his lifestyle, he moved to the Continent, where he smuggled drugs and arms on a run between Malta, North Africa and Spain. He spent time in a string of foreign jails.

He married 17-year old Vera, the daughter of his mother's friend, Mrs Bonner. Over the years the couple separated and divorce proceedings were set in motion. The only way John Donald Merrett could get his money back was if she predeceased him. During the war he was described as hard drinking, 6ft tall and weighing 22st with a huge black beard; he also had a large gold earring in his right ear and a Cyrano de Bergerac of a nose. In the war he somehow managed to force his way into the Royal Navy and skippered motor boats in the Mediterranean. He could not miss an opportunity to evade the law with his activities and he smuggled contraband into Italy. After the war, he changed his name to Ronald Chesney and when his money ran out, he moved to Germany. Living on the Continent, Chesney used a stolen passport to make an undetected return to England, and found Vera was living with her mother. He drowned his wife in the bath, and when her mother arrived home, Chesney strangled her. Realising he would be caught and face the hangman, he escaped back to Germany, went into the woods and shot himself.

As for Paul Dukes; he moved to Helsingfors and saw a picture in the barbers of a smart looking man with a goatee beard. Shorn of his greasy locks and shabby dress, Dukes departed the barbers in Helsingfors looking more like a well-groomed individual. He moved on to Stockholm, where he spent Christmas with his bureau chief, John Scale, and his wife. He wired London with the copious information of Bolshevik Russia and informed Mansfield Cumming that he was returning to Petrograd.

# Chapter Six

# Lieutenant Augustus Agar

One midwinter day, the Osea Island establishment received a visit from an unnamed bemonacled naval commander, who walked with a pronounced limp. He was most interested in the performance and capabilities of the Coastal Motor Boats and their great turn of speed. He asked Lieutenant Augustus Agar several questions but gave nothing away as to the purpose of his visit. The limping commander was Mansfield Smith-Cumming, the head of the Secret Intelligence Service (MI6), who returned to London with his mind made up of the wooden-framed 'skimmers'. Paul Dukes was his agent in Petrograd but the length of time it took to get information from the city via his couriers was too long and he sought a quicker method.

In September 1918 the British decided to send a force to the ports of Murmansk and Archangel in Northern Russia to reclaim the supplies left at the docks. In doing so, Britain became embroiled in a short, fruitless and largely forgotten conflict, which, nonetheless, produced five VC actions. The cessation of hostilities did not bring peace to Europe but stirred up conflict for social change and national identity. The struggle for Russia between the Bolsheviks and the White Russians had encouraged the Baltic States of Estonia, Latvia, Lithuania, Poland and Finland, all former Russian provinces, to declare their independence in 1917 and 1918. With the exception of Finland, the other states were grabbed by the Soviet Union after the Second World War until the 1990s, when they became independent.

The Bolsheviks had become very wary of foreigners and frequently attacked them in the streets. Strangely enough, Arthur Ransome, correspondent for the *Daily News*, enjoyed a good relationship with Lenin and would frequently visit him. As a writer, he said he would write the history of the Bolsheviks and their history, something that Lenin was supportive of. Although a left-winger, he spied for Cumming but was lambasted by his critics at home. Finally, the Foreign Office closed their embassies in Petrograd and Moscow, but kept their Chancelleries open to enable their agents to feed back intelligence.

Augustus Willington Agar was the youngest of thirteen children born to Irishman John Shelton Agar, from Woodmount, County Kerry, and Emily, his Austrian wife. In 1860 his father left Ireland with plans to start a tea plantation in Ceylon, Sri Lanka. He took with him a pack of hunting dogs so he might pursue animals apart from foxes. All the Agar children were born in Ceylon, and Augustus – or Gus as he was more generally called – was born in Kandy, Ceylon on 4 January 1890. A combination of excessive childbirth and the tropical climate carried away Emily as soon as Gus was born. His father was left to bring up his large family the best he could by sending his boys to an English boarding school and his girls to either Vienna or Germany. As the youngest, Gus' turn came when he was 8 years old and he was sent with his brother John on a long voyage to England. After an idyllic childhood of being looked after by servants in a lush tropical paradise, young Gus came down to earth with a thud when he joined his first boarding school in East Anglia in the middle of winter. Cold, miserable and inept at sports, Gus somehow adjusted to his new life.

During holidays, he and other fellow boarders whose parents were overseas were sent to vicarages near the seaside. It was here he got his first taste of the sea; he enjoyed sailing and the occasional trip in a fishing boat. When he was 12, he learned that his father had contracted cholera in China and died. From the boarding school he moved to Framingham College in Suffolk and was cared for by his disabled elder brother, Shelton, who took over the responsibility of raising Gus, becaming more like a father to him. Without consultation, it was decided by Shelton and the Trustees that Gus should go into the Royal Navy. He had no particular inclination to do so, but showed willingness to please his beloved oldest brother. Sir Henry Jackson, a friend of the family and later First Sea Lord, nominated Gus for the annual intake of cadets.

Leaving Framingham College, he was sent to a 'crammer' at Eastman's Naval Academy. At the age of 13 he passed his entrance exam and entered HMS *Brittania;* the last batch to go through this illustrious old training ship before all the cadets moved onshore to the newly-built Dartmouth College. Here he found the family he had been missing and he revelled in navy life. As part of the training, Agar was a cadet on the second-rate cruiser, HMS *Highflyer* and afterwards on the slightly older HMS *Isis*. Both these ships were stationed at Bermuda, and the cadets had to sit their classes when the ships were in port.

In 1905 he passed his examinations and received his first seagoing appointment on HMS *Prince of Wales*. Between 1906 and 1910, Gus served on four ships, including HMS *Queen*. The latter was commanded by Captain (later Admiral) David Beatty, whom he greatly admired for his dash and style. In 1911, he scraped though his exams and became acting sub-lieutenant in the 'Small Ship Navy', which was regarded as rather unglamorous. Gus, however, enjoyed serving on a series of torpedo boats and destroyers. His first ship was the *Ruby*, a torpedo destroyer. These smaller ships were more independent and relaxed than the more rigid regimes of the capital ships. He spent the next period on a course at Portsmouth and studying at the Royal Navy College, Greenwich. He was promoted to lieutenant on 30 June 1912 and was assigned to Torpedo Boat No. 23.

In 1913 he attempted to become an aviator and joined the Central Flying School at Upavon. In what was something of a surprise, the Admiralty had given their blessing to those officers who wished to learn to fly, with the proviso that there would be no flying on Sundays. In the process of attaining his pilot's license, Agar wrote off three aircraft without seriously injuring himself. On being transferred to Commander Charles Samson's section, the new leader of the Royal Navy Air Service (RNAS) decided that Agar should return to sea duties rather than fly. Despite the rebuff, Agar remained a firm advocate of a naval air arm. This was more than could be said for the then Secretary of State for War, who declared that 'the government do not consider that aeroplanes will be of any possible use for war purposes'.

In September 1913, he joined the old pre-dreadnought battleship, HMS *Hibernia*. As newer dreadnoughts joined the fleet, the older battleships became increasingly obsolete, being slower and with less firepower. When the war broke out in August 1914, *Hibernia* sailed north to join the Grand Fleet at Scapa Flow, where they expected an attack by the German High Seas Fleet. This did not happen and *Hibernia* and other pre-dreadnoughts were ordered to sail to the Dardanelles in the early summer of 1915 in support of the army which had landed on the Gallipoli side. For two months, the *Hibernia* cruised up and down the

Turkish coast firing salvoes from her 6-inch guns and only once was she struck by a Turkish shell which did little damage. For the first time in his life, Gus experienced the incoming fire when the Turkish sent a shell through one of the funnels. Although the older ships were either sunk or did little damage, the campaign was a costly failure. Finally, the army pulled out of Gallipoli with *Hibernia* and other pre-dreadnoughts helping to cover the evacuation.

Returning to British waters, the old ship was anchored off Sheerness to protect the Thames Estuary; a monotonous and thankless duty that Agar had to put up with until he was transferred. In early 1917, he was transferred as second in command of the ancient light cruiser *Iphigenia*, which was sent to the Northern Russian port of Murmansk to act as a floating base for the fleet of British mine sweepers. They were tasked with keeping the sea lanes open as the mine sweepers cleared the German mines; again, another thankless task. *Iphigenia* had arrived in March 1917 just as the Russian Revolution started. She operated from Archangel in the summer when the White Sea was clear of ice and at Murmansk during the winter. Although the material was still being sent to Russia, the local Allied commanders were unable to stop the flow from the civil servants in Whitehall. Most of the supplies were either used by the Bolsheviks or the Germans. Revolution had broken out and piles of war material were left on the Murmansk docks to either be stolen or rotted away.

Agar was able to renew acquaintanceships with some of the officers he had served with in the Dardanelles when he was on the *Hibernia*, and met them again at Devonport dockyard. Agar was promoted to executive officer on *Iphigenia*, and adjacent to their anchorage was the five-funnelled Russian cruiser, *Askold*. He witnessed the spectacle of sailors mutinying against their officers, most of whom were taken ashore and shot. The sailors stayed on board, listening to revolutionary speeches and generally loafing about until the food and drink ran out. The ship was abandoned and within a couple of months the *Askold* had become a rusting derelict. The Navy had orders not to intervene, as the new Social Revolutionary Government under Alexander Kerensky had promised to continue the war against Germany, which was all that concerned Britain and the Allies. As the year passed, it became clear even to a naval officer in the remote White Sea that Russia was in turmoil. By the end of February 1918, the worsening conditions and a hostile Bolshevik government prompted a withdrawal. In the teeth of below-zero temperatures, the British managed to smuggle out several Russian refugees from the Bolsheviks. The supplies from Britain continued to pile up on the dockside, where they were either looted or decayed.

Finally, word was received that the Kerensky government had been ousted by the Bolsheviks and that another civil war had broken out. The new regime wanted to gain complete control without the distraction of fighting the Germans, and began to negotiate a separate peace. At the end of February 1918, the *Iphigenia* sailed out of the White Sea, following a Canadian icebreaker though the thick ice, and headed for her home port of Chatham. Here, *Iphigenia* would find one last glorious task waiting for her. Her age made her available as one of the blockships that were sunk at the entrance of the canal that opened into the port of Zeebrugge.

After a short leave, Agar was summoned to the Admiralty, where he found he had been selected to do a special course in mining, as he had had some experience during his service on the *Iphigenia*. It turned out that this was just part of his appointment and in 1917 a new and exciting warship was about to enter service, and Gus' rather low-key war was about change. He was transferred to a new and secret naval establishment being constructed on the 600-acre Osea Island, which stands at the mouth of the Blackwater River in Essex. The navy shared this remote island with a farmer, so there was quite a menagerie of chickens, ducks and pigs. This isolated position was chosen as the base for two special high-speed craft known as Coastal Motor Boats (CMBs), which had been developed by Sir John Thornycroft. The boats were powered by 250-brake-horsepower V-12 aircraft engines made by Sunbeam and Napier, but later used the engines of Greens and Thornycroft. They had a monocoque construction, with a skeleton of Honduran mahogany backed by oil-soaked calico, which fed oil to the wood to prevent it from drying out. The CMBs had a hydroplane–type hull, which skimmed over the water when driven at high speed (40 knots) and which gave them a shallow draft of about 3ft. At these speeds they could travel over the minefields with impunity, unless they hit a mine that had come adrift. They could be armed with a torpedo, depth charges or used as minelayers, and could reach enemy targets that conventional ships could not. Five boats were lost and they were dangerous and difficult to handle due to their petrol-driven engines being prone to catching fire.

There were two sizes; the smaller, 40ft one carried one torpedo, while the 55ft one could take two. These could not be fired from forward-facing tubes but carried in a rear-mounted trough. On launching, the torpedo was pushed backwards by a cordite firing pistol and a steel ram. They entered the water tailfirst, and a tripwire between the torpedo and the ram head would start the torpedo motor once pulled tight after release. The CMB would then turn hard over and get out of the way of the torpedo; there has never been an instance of a CMB being torpedoed.

It was planned for Agar to command a flotilla to carry and lay the top-secret magnetic mines outside the enemy harbours in Belgium. A mining course at Portsmouth was followed with a highly enjoyable few weeks at Dunkirk, where he learned how to operate these revolutionary boats. They were not comfortable and the driving position was exposed to freezing seawater being thrown by the bow waves. He was at Dunkirk when the famous St George's Day Raid on Zeebrugge was ordered. The CMBs were selected to lay smoke screens outside the Zeebrugge mole to cover the escape of the crews of the blockships. Although he did not take part in the actual raid, Agar viewed the attack from one of the spare boats. One of the blockships that had been sunk at the entrance to the canal was Agar's old ship, *Iphigenia*. Unfortunately, they sank the old ship in such a way that the German U-boats were able to manoeuvre around the obstacle.

HMS *Osea's* commanding officer, Captain Wilfred French, had originally recruited Gus to the CMB service, as he was an expert in mines and torpedoes and was referred to as 'the torpedo conscript'. They struck up a friendship and French promised Gus that he would be given command of the new 70ft CMB. Sadly it was put on hold while other 40ft and 55ft CMBs were sent to Archangel, Riga, the Caspian Sea and the Rhine. He was kept back as he was the only officer with knowledge of the mines and torpedoes that the CMBs carried. Plans were then made for the CMBs to mount a raid on the High Seas Fleet. The German ships were lying in anchor in the Tershilling Roads, but by the declaration of the November Armistice, the attack was shelved. Although Agar was happy to be attached to the CMBs, he felt somewhat deflated that he had not had a chance to taste the thrill of battle and there was a sense of anti-climax amongst the Osea Island sailors.

In February 1919 Lieutenant Agar received a summons to report to the Naval Intelligence Division at the Admiralty. There was little happening at Osea Island, so he relished the thought of joining the Intelligence Division. Arriving at the Admiralty, he was walked round to Horse Guards and No. 2, Whitehall Court. Taken to the top floor by a female staff member, he began a long walk through a maze of corridors, which culminated in a bridge on the rooftop and ended up in the office of the Chief of SIS. On entering, he recognised the mystery naval officer, Mansfield Cumming, who had visited Osea Island a few weeks earlier. Agar was asked to sign the Official Secrets Act that introduced him into the pay of the Secret Service. Before any details were discussed, the limping naval officer outlined that communications with their 'top man' had broken down and it was essential to restore them. The person he chose for the task was Lieutenant Augustus Agar. He was staying at the Waldorf Hotel when he got a telephone message from Cumming saying that he wanted Agar immediately. Agar was excited by the summons and later wrote: 'I was still keen to take part in more of our war activities … It meant excitement, adventure and sometimes out of the ordinary dull routine.'

He asked Chief Motor Mechanic Hugh Beeley for his assessment of a couple of CMBs. He chose *CMB-4*, which had some success at the closing stages of the war. Beeley also chose *CMB-7*, which had torpedoed another German warship on 30 April. The commander of the four CMBs was Lieutenant Walter Beckett, who went hunting for German ships off the Weilingen Channel at Zeebrugge. On 7 April 1918, he pursued one destroyer and managed to sink her. He also damaged another and was awarded the Distinguished Service Cross. Agar was informed that the mysterious agent was known by the code name 'ST25', the last British agent left in Russia. The ST identification was used for all Russian operations and was used by Stockholm's Baltic area. He was informed by Cumming that: 'Soviet Russia was a closed book and a hostile country with which we were virtually at war … a certain Englishman – unnamed, and with regard to whom no details were given – who remained in Russia to conduct Intelligence, whose work was regarded of vital importance and with whom it was essential to get in touch … as he was the only man who had first hand reliable information on certain things which required urgently by our government.'

They discussed the speed of the CMBs that they were to use, and with the Gulf of Finland lavishly sown with mines, Cumming suggested that the 'skimmers' would easily rise above the mines. The 40ft long CMB was made of a wooden skeleton, with canvas stretched over the frame; they were powered by a Thornycroft engine, with FIAT and other aircraft engines available. Low in the water, it was the ideal craft to deliver and collect couriers offshore from north Petrograd. The craft could reach speeds of 40mph, skimming above the mines which the Bolsheviks had sown to the west of Kronstadt harbour. It was stressed that no torpedoes were to be used and it was pointed out that Agar and his companions would no longer belong to the Royal Navy but were transferred to the Secret Service. They would adopt civilian identities and wear non-uniform clothing, but they could – if they were captured – revert to their naval uniforms. This was soon altered. Agar, his crew of five, and their the two boats were now technically under the command of the Foreign Office. The British government was without a firm and clear policy, but the Secret Service was virtually given free rein to obtain information on developments in Russia. For such clandestine operations, the British Government would deny any responsibility if they were captured.

The Gulf of Finland is about 250 miles long but only 30 miles wide. As one approached Petrograd, Kotlin Island stood mid-channel, 5 miles long and 1 mile wide. There were sea fortresses running from the north of the island and were linked by a hidden breakwater, 3ft below the surface of the water. Some fortresses were on the Kotlin Island, with five guarding the entrance to the harbour. The fortresses to the south were not linked by breakwaters, and they commanded the narrow deepwater channel guarded by an extensive minefield. The Bolsheviks had disabled the mines' safety devices and if they broke free, they were a hazard to most shipping. On the Estonian shore stood the fortress Krasnaya Gorka (Little Pea) in the hands of the White Army but manned by Ingranians, a population based on Estonians living near the Baltic. Nearer Petrograd stood the Oranienbaum seaplane base and the whole area south was patrolled by motor patrol boats and aircraft.

Having been instructed how to navigate the northbound fortresses, Agar returned by train to Maldon and by taxi onto Osea Island. He explained to his friend, Captain Wilfred French, the top-secret mission in the Baltic that he was about to undergo. His first priority was to pick five young, unmarried men; Sub-Lieutenants John White Hampsheir and Edgar 'Sinbad' Sindall, and Midshipmen Richard Nigel Onslow Marshall. In addition, he took two mechanics, one for each boat; Chief Motor Mechanics Hugh Beeley for *CMB-4* and Albert Victor Piper for *CMB-7*. There was one other engineer, Richard Pegler, at Helsingfors, to help with the engines but who would not be involved in the work of the couriers. Two days later Agar was back in 'C's office, explaining his plans.

# Chapter Seven

# Dukes' Second Visit

Having accompanied his small group from Petrograd to the Finnish border, Paul Dukes spent time changing his appearance. He travelled to Helsingfors and went to the barbers, carrying an advertisement showing a Frenchman with a smart goatee and a trim haircut. He told the barber that was just what he wanted to look like. Looking smarter, he spent Christmas with the Scales at Stockholm, sending his intelligence to London before returning to Helsingfors. He used his more urbane appearance and was known as Sergei Ilitch, a Serb commercial traveller, and he gave the appearance of a salesman. Ten days after he crossed the border into Finland, he returned to Raiaioki and met up with his frontier guards. Waiting until midnight, he chose the name Joseph Krylenko and was given documents to see him through to Petrograd. Walking about 2 miles upstream, he found the Sestro River frozen. One of the guards gave him a large white sheet; in case he was spotted, he could hide beneath it.

He crossed the icebound stream easily enough and climbed the meadow to the lane, where he found the same half-built house to take shelter in. With the first streaks of dawn, he discarded the white sheet and strode to the station, where he bought a ticket to Petrograd. Yet again, he found a different feeling in Petrograd; the city that the Bolsheviks proudly entitled 'Metropolis of the World Revolution'. The Communists had taken over the people's cooperative societies and trade unions, and ruled them with rigid control. While he patiently listened for the umpteenth time to the Policeman's accounts of how he had shaken hands with the Tsar, who had kissed every member of his household down to the last stable boy, and was duly rewarded by the Tsar. In the snow-bound streets of Petrograd at the beginning of February 1919, he finally found out from the Policeman what had happened to Melnikov. He had been shot by the Cheka while in captivity, between the 15 and 20 January. Dukes was stunned by Melnikov's death, having firmly counted on him as an accomplice in his gathering of intelligence.

Dukes later met up with Zorinsky, who invited him to dinner with his actress wife, Elena Ivanovna, who wanted to know if Finland was in a better situation for food than Russia. Dukes laid it on; he told them there was plenty to eat, drawing a comprehensive list of delicacies unavailable in Russia. He also presented Elena Ivanovna with a bouquet of flowers, thanking her for the dinner she had prepared. Over coffee, Zorinsky thrust a large blue sheet of paper into Dukes' hands. The sheet showed a sketch of the Finnish Gulf, and in one corner was the words, *Fortress of Kronstadt, Distribution of Mines.* This was a plan of the minefield to the west of Kronstadt with the mines submerged 6ft beneath the surface of the sea. This prevented Admiral Walter Cowan's Fleet from approaching Kronstadt and they had to exchange fire from a long distance. The only vessel to approach Kronstadt was the Coastal Motor Boat; its depth was 2ft 9in, but it was notoriously prone to breakdowns by the seas that surrounded. How Zorinsky came by this blueprint, Dukes did not know. He was given one evening to copy it and return it to Zorinsky in the morning. Dukes sent the detailed drawing of the minefield by courier to London. He prevented the Royal Navy ever attacking Kronstadt, possibly saving many ships and men.

Zorinsky worked for both sides. He was in contact with the Cheka and it soon become apparent that he had a shady reputation. This was a good enough reason to leave Russia and this put Dukes in a quandary, for he had to get out of Petrograd immediately. Dukes wrote,

> I have not the slightest doubt now that I all but fell an early victim of this mode of operation, though in my case the climax may have been delayed and my life saved because Zorinsky wanted first to get as much money out of me as possible. But I am certain that if I remained in Russia another week at that moment I should not have lived to tell the tale.

In addition to the blueprint, Zorinsky later also handed Dukes a newly procured exemption certificate stating that he suffered from an incurable heart disease and therefore was excused from military service. When he left the Zorinsky house, he went to one of his safe houses. As he sat and contemplated the exemption certificate, he was surprised to find out that the form was stuck together with a blank. He realised that he now had two exemptions. He made his way to the hospital where he met 'the Doctor' – a relative of Melnikov – who managed to find another passport. Dukes was able to insert his false name of Joseph Krylenko, and within days, he 'lost' his passport. Shura Marenko, a friend of the Doctor, had acquired another passport, which was also lost on a visit to Moscow. The new exemption form was written out in the name of 'Alexander Markovich', a postal office clerk, another one of Dukes' several aliases. Dukes made the acquaintance of a commissar investigator who boasted of his connection with the Cheka and managed to persuade a couple to get the Cheka man drunk to the extent that he quit his position and became a 'professional agitator.'

> Two of my assistants, having obtained a bottle of vodka one day, got him drunk and persuaded him to tell of some of the methods at Gorohovaya. He said that in case the authorities felt that a victim was concealing something from them, they would apply methods of torture. The torture consisted in the rapid and consistent firing of revolvers where the victim was sitting; the feeding of the prisoners for days on nothing but salt herrings, but refusing to give him water to drink; flogging and the application of red hot needles to the quick of the fingers 'It got on my nerve' said this Communist testily 'that I gave up that job and became a professional agitator'.

Another old friend was Miss Laura Ann Cade, who taught languages. She was a member of the Petrograd Guild of English Teachers, a social club for tutors and governesses. The guild organised parties and staged plays and reviews. Due to the Bolsheviks taking control, the guild had shrunk. Dukes had known Laura Cade from when he joined the Conservator around 1912. He turned up in his ruffian-like disguise and Miss Cade was taken aback by his appearance, but readily agreed to store his reports hidden in the old text books that adorned the walls. Paul Dukes was warned to stay away by the flowerpot missing from her window, and in December 1919 – as part of the roundup of Dukes' suspects – she was arrested but managed to escape. Dukes sent Peter Petrovich into Petrograd in February 1920 to get her out. He appeared at her flat one evening and told her to put her belongings in a suitcase, then smuggled her out the same night in a sleigh across the frozen Gulf of Finland. She managed to cross the Finnish frontier and – like Dukes – she suffered frostbite but did manage to reach England. She was accompanied by a Russian woman, who escaped with her. She settled down in the village of Littlebury, near Saffron Walden, until the 1950s. Some remember her as a very rich woman or as a companion to a lady who was wealthy.

Paul Dukes' association with Captain Zorinsky was a fragile one for he was convinced that the unreliable Zorinsky was part of the Cheka. Although the Policeman was a mercenary but trustworthy, Zorinsky was a confirmed member of the Cheka, who held out for money. Zorinsky often referred to Melnikov's sister and Dukes had paid money to help with Melnikov's sister. It was not until he found out that Zorinsky had lied about Melnikov's having a sibling that he decided to break all connections with this scoundrel. The Doctor dismissed the 'sister' as fabrication and persuaded Dukes that Zorinsky was after money.

Dukes travelled to the hospital, which was some distance from the centre of the city. He met and grown attached to the Doctor, whose name Dukes did not disclose. Dukes' attendances at Bolshevik meetings were pointless as they were repetitious, but he made haste to attend the Communist gathering at the Winter Palace. A small group of Bolsheviks was gathered around the base of the tall obelisk in the middle of Palace Square, surrounded by two rows of soldiers, including Dmitri, the nephew of Stepanovna. Dukes recognised him, made sure he was not spotted and moved away. After bearing the intense cold, during which several orators declared their love at length of the communist doctrine, a car drew up and Zinoviev, the President of the Petrograd Soviet alighted. He was one of the greatest orators of the Communist Party and the President of the Third International that would affect the world's revolution. His oratorical skills were crude, which appealed to the small crowd, and due to the bitter cold getting to him, he soon retreated to his car and drove off. By 1916 Zinoviev had become a major figure but still a great speaker, being thin and a firebrand, but several years of fattening changed him into becoming obese.

It was the beginning of February that Dukes saw Stepanovna for the last time. He found that Varia had been arrested trying to communicate with Ivan Sergeievich in Finland and that she had gone to the Finland Station and was arrested on the train. Dukes arranged a meeting with Stepanovna in the Kazan Cathedral and the next day stood on the corner of the street to observe the housekeeper. He spotted the housekeeper emerge from the apartment and head for the cathedral. In the gloom of the cathedral, he saw her make for the altar, fall on her knees and pray. It was the last time he saw her.

The next day Dukes met with the Doctor who told him that Melnikov's friend, Shura, had investigated Zorinsky and found that he was in close contact with No. 2 Gorohovaya. Dukes had two couriers from Finland but only one produced a cipher message which was indecipherable. Sending the messenger back to Finland, it was now time for Dukes to leave Petrograd and visit Helsingfors. Having closed all contacts for the next few weeks, he made his way to Staraya Derevnya, a run-down northern island known as 'the Old Village' overlooking the Gulf of Petrograd. It was a poor, shabby locality with timber yards, log-men's huts and second-rate summer villas made all the worse by the biting winds and the expanse of ice.

He had sent off some of his couriers with messages and intelligence to Helsingfors for forwarding to London. He also felt it was time he should get away while the Cheka were searching for him. He joined a Finnish smuggler and together they rested in the small hut by the shore until midnight. Dukes waited with his smuggler until the night became dark enough that they could take the *drovny,* a low broad sleigh filled with hay, onto the ice. Within moments they were moving at speed across the ice and soon could make out Kronstadt. Once past the northern forts, they were home and dry. As they passed Lissy Nos, the narrowest part of the strait, they spotted a group of five horsemen emerging from the pine forest and coming in pursuit after them. They tried to increase the distance but the horsemen drew closer. Dukes used his revolver to fire at the pursing horsemen but the sleigh swung about so much that the smuggler had difficulty with his reins as they were caught in the shafts. Suddenly the horse fell and the sleigh overturned, throwing both passengers out. Dukes sprang up and immediately made a run for the shore, keeping clear of the big patch of windswept ice. Looking back, he saw the horsemen capture the smuggler. He spotted a broad, snow-free patch and lay down on the black ice. Motionless, he heard the groaning sounds of water beneath the ice. To act as if he was a smuggler, he threw his intelligence documents and maps away and lay still. The riders were unable to see much with the dark skies and black ice and kept to the snowy patches. At last, the horsemen gave up the chase and returned to the sleigh and the captured smuggler. Gathering up his reports, Dukes was all alone on the ice with only a vague idea as to how to reach the Finnish shore. Without skis, he stumbled and fell over during the next six hours and heard the sea murmuring beneath the ice. While cursing the frozen ice, he heard a man coming the other way. Dukes found a black patch of ice to lie down on again, while the silhouette passed by, stumbling and swearing, without spotting Dukes. Having spent hours stumbling amongst the ice floes, Dukes finally reached the shore but was unable to find whether he was in Russia or Finland. He spotted a sign which showed he was in Finland and he soon found a hut to rest behind. He was discovered by the Finnish guards before long. He was taken to Terrioki, a couple of miles inland from the yacht club, and placed in a cell. The pro-German commandant was obnoxious but allowed him to make one call to the British legation in Helsingfors and – after much discussion – he was freed. Making his way to the station, he caught a train to Helsingfors. He met up with John Scales and had the satisfaction of hearing that his intelligence gathering had satisfied London. The pro-German commandant at the fort of Terrioki had been fed information that Dukes was visiting Helsingfors to complain to the Interior Minister about the treatment he had received from the commandant. While in Helsingfors, Dukes managed to obtain documents from the Finnish War Ministry and put the word about that he was planning to return to Petrograd via sleigh or skis. The commandant issued orders that anyone on the ice should be fired upon. Within a week, Dukes was making his way back into Petrograd for the third and last time.

Instead of travelling on the ice, Dukes planned to travel some 40 miles north to reach a remote village named Rautta close to the border. In a roundabout railway journey, he met up with a young officer who was to take up duties as commander of the small garrison in the village. Showing the papers from the War Ministry, he asked the young officer to arrange for a guide to take him across the border. Dukes realised that he needed a longer pair of skis to make any progress but he was given a shorter pair instead. After a long journey, the guide and Dukes managed to reach the frontier. With dawn breaking and seeing nobody about, the guide took a run; he prodded his sticks into the bank and lifted himself across the brook. The heavily-clad Dukes tried the same and ended up in the water.

When he managed to clamber up the bank, he saw that from the waist down he was completely frozen over. The guide had long gone ahead and Dukes was at the brink of exhaustion. Removing most of the ice from his overcoat, he realised that he was suffering from frostbite on his feet, caused by the freezing water. As he could not treat this, for the next few days he had to suffer while he made the long journey to Petrograd. Although a long way behind his Finnish guide, he managed to reach a hamlet of a few peasant cottages, one of which belonged to an old man named Uncle Egor.

Thoroughly exhausted, Dukes stumbled into one of the peasants' houses. The first thing he noticed was an old harmonium with only the top notes playable. The old man welcomed Dukes into his hut and Egor introduced him to his wife, daughter and grandchildren. Egor sat down to play some hymns and Dukes offered to play few simple tunes, which captivated the old man. Instead of being sullen, the old man welcomed Dukes' playing; he became effusive and invited Dukes to dinner for a bowl of sour cabbage soup. Exhausted by his journey, Dukes fell into a deep sleep but was roused by his Finnish guide, who managed to find him. Fully awake, he travelled to a small wayside station at Toksova with Uncle Egor and one of his daughters, who joined many other peasants anxious to sell their wares to the inhabitants of Petrograd. Halfway to Petrograd, the train ground to a halt and word was passed that the Red Guards had entered the train and were checking papers. In fact, they were only looking for food but in the mayhem many of the peasants escaped via the windows and doors. Dukes and his companions remained and eventually the train set off and arrived at Okhta Station on the east side of the city. The Red Guards were lined up, waiting to grab the peasants' goods. The mass panic that unfolded caused the guards to fire in the air. Women and children were pushed to the ground and trampled underfoot, while the men ran in different directions. In the melee, Dukes was swept along by the crowd and he managed to escape by crossing the Okhta Bridge and disappearing in the side streets. Having lost Egor and his daughter, Dukes stumbled along in agony from the frostbite and made for the centre of the Petrograd. There seemed to be many Mongolian and Lettish troops who were stopping the pedestrians and stealing anything of value from them.

Now in great pain, he made for his nearest safe house; one belonging to a Russian civil servant. Waiting for half an hour in the freezing cold, he decided to take a chance and ask for refuge. As he climbed the stairs, he heard the Russian word for 'lockpick'. Turning, he accidentally stumbled onto a pile of loose tiles, which aroused the Cheka. Unable to make his escape, he was caught by an officer of the Cheka wearing a leather jacket and two belts of cartridges, who demanded to know what he was doing in the building. Using a pathetic story, Dukes managed to shuffle away from the officer, who went back inside.

Stumbling along, he barely managed to reach the Doctor. Exhausted, his boots were cut off, taking with it a great deal of skin. His toes looked black and rotten, and the Doctor advised him to stay in the hospital for several weeks until he was able to walk. Instead, Dukes only stayed for a couple of days, rested and in agony from frostbite.

# Chapter Eight

# Agar Searches For a Base

Gus Agar was given the code number 'ST34' and was told that the Stockholm office would help him plan his mission. The problem of the couriers was soon to be addressed in the spring by Mansfield Cumming on a visit to Osea Island. Special measures were being devised to solve the problem of communication, and the CMBs were the answer. On Sunday, 25 May 1919, Gus' crew were aboard the old Swedish steamer SS *Fennia* at Tynemouth, facing a stormy passage to Stockholm. Bedevilled with sea sickness and with very little to do except play cards, the journey seemed to take forever. The machine guns and the torpedo-firing gear were stripped and packed separately, and the two CMBs were resplendent in brilliant white instead of the dull grey. When they arrived in Sweden, everything seemed to go wrong. They were held up by the Swedish Customs, who questioned their implausible cover story that the vessels were the latest type of pleasure boats and the crew were actually salesmen. In a rush to catch the railway to Helsingfors (later Helsinki), they were told the train was leaving at 7.10 am the following day. Somehow the stationmaster had given Gus the wrong information and they had to wait until the following day before they could travel to Helsingfors. Reaching the capital in the early hours of Sunday morning, Gus visited the British Consul and told them of their courier service, the *Fennia*'s carrying petrol and oil, and the location of the nearest inlet to Russia. SS *Pallux* had lifted the two CMBs on deck and, together with Sindall, Piper and another mechanic named Richard Pegler, sailed to Helsingfors. It was suggested that a destroyer should tow the CMBs from Helsingfors to Biorko but this soon caused problems due to seawater entering the engine room and affecting the balance of the engine. This led to the stripping of the engines at Biorko, which took some considerable time.

Gus' other supporter was the commander of the Royal Navy Force in the Baltic, Rear-Admiral Walter Cowan. He had replaced Rear-

Admiral Alexander-Sinclair and took command of the 1st Light Cruiser Squadron (*Inconstant, Galatea, Phaeton, Royalist* and *Caledon*). After the Armistice, the Baltic states of Estonia, Finland, Latvia and Lithuania declared their independence from both Germany and Russia. The Allies were quick to recognise the newly independent countries but were slow to supply them with material aid. Forming a backup, the V and W destroyers were the latest class from the First World War. At the time they were the most powerful and advanced ships of their type in the world. They were supported by minesweepers, auxiliary cargo vessels and the converted cruiser was renamed *Vindictive,* after originally being launched as *Cavendish.* She was altered to be one of the first aircraft carriers and in a few weeks, she was ready for service by the end of the war. She took part in the Baltic campaign against the Bolsheviks and her hotchpotch of aircraft took part in numerous attacks against the naval base at Kronstadt. She was skippered by Captain Edgar 'Dasher' Grace, the son of renowned cricketer W.G. Grace. This new conversion to an aircraft carrier carried a few obsolete aircraft that were wary of landing on a short landing deck. While at Revel, she ran aground on a shoal just outside the port. Jettisoning her fuel and ammunition, it took eight days with the efforts of *Danae* and *Cleopatra,* together with three tugs, to pull her off the shoal. While they attempted this operation, they were blissfully unaware they were surrounded by a minefield.

On 17 May the Bolsheviks tried a reconnaissance-in-force out of their base, in which a heavy destroyer accompanied by four other vessels was supported by the *Petropavlovsk* and *Oleg,* who fired from outside the harbour. The destroyers moved to the edge of the minefield and exchanged fire with the British cruisers. One of the British shells hit the Bolshevik destroyer, which slowed her to a few knots but she managed to slink back into Kronstadt harbour. Cowan pursued as far as he dared, but the 12in guns mounted at Kronstadt fortresses caused him to retreat.

In 1868 John Murray published a series of books, including *Handbook for Travellers in Russia,* in which he wrote about Kronstadt,

The fortifications are extensive and were begun by Peter the Great in 1793. Prince Menshikov constructed the works under the direction of Peter and one of the forts still bears his name. Succeeding governments have strengthened the fortifications and secured the approaches from seaward by sinking ships and erecting batteries, especially after the visit of the Baltic squadrons in 1854. It has been the chief station in the Baltic for the Russian Fleet. The dry docks will admit the largest vessels of war, and the splendid steam factory almost rivals Keyham (Plymouth) in its mechanical appliances.

Kronstadt was to the Russian Navy what Portsmouth was to the British. Kotlin Island was the largest of the islands in the Gulf of Finland, being well defended by fortresses extending north and south. Conveniently sited 15 miles from Petrograd, its eight forts had been supplemented by a chain of nine fortresses extending across a 6-mile-wide channel to the north. To the south, a channel had been dug to allow merchant shipping to enter and exit. Six forts had been built across 4 miles to prevent any incursion by enemy ships, which rendered Petrograd virtually impregnable. On the two countries, Estonia and Krasnaya Gorka look north to Kotlin Isand while further along, Fort Ino on the Finnish side looked south.

In 1919 the Russian naval base at Kronstadt was probably the best-protected fleet base in the world, and behind the island that lay across was the entrance to Petrograd. The Bolshevik Baltic Fleet consisted of the dreadnought *Petropavlovsk*, the pre-dreadnought *Andrei Pervozvanny*, the armoured cruiser *Oleg*, six heavy destroyers, *Gavrill, Azard, Konstantin, Svobada, Spartak*, and *Avtroil*, and four light destroyers, *Vsadnik, Gaigamak, Amuretz*, and *Ussurietz*. Moored inside the harbour was obsolete cruiser *Rurik*, which carried some 300 mines, with which she was about to extend the minefield. Later, Commander 'Tommy' (Claude) Dobson cautioned about torpedoing this deadly cargo but suggested that the last CMB should fire its torpedo while the rest of the flotilla moved out of range. Added to these vessels were a flotilla of submarines, numerous patrol boats and a seaplane base at Oranienbaum on the southern Russian shore. Wisely, Admiral Cowan decided to move his fleet from Reval to Biorko Sound, off the Finnish coast, and keep an eye on any activity around Kronstadt.

Converted cruiser *Vindictive* had been sent to the Baltic with a mixture of aircraft, comprising of Griffins, Sopwith 2F.1 Fighters, 1½ Strutter and Short Type 184 fighters, which proved handy for an attack on Kronstadt harbour. As a lowly lieutenant, Gus Agar asked Admiral Cowan for a couple of ratings to be attached to his command to deal with the cooking and guard duty. Cowan had taken a shine to Agar and complied with his request.

The brilliant white of the two CMBs soon changed to a light grey colour as it was unlikely that impoverished Finland could afford the cost of two very fast speedboats. Gus always remembered Cowan's words; 'Nothing is worthwhile doing unless there is a risk to it. Always choose the boldest course if you have any choice at all; it is always the boldest course that stands the best chance of success.'

Before transferring his squadron, Cowan had a meeting in Reval. He sent the destroyer *Vanessa,* to pick up Gus, John Scale and a couple of Finnish ministers from Helsingfors to Reval. Transferring to the cruiser *Cleopatra,* Gus had to wait some eight hours for Walter Cowan to complete his lunch and meeting. In the meantime, Gus met a very tall Russian named Pyotr Sokolov, the main courier for Paul Dukes. Peter, as he was better known, was 28 years old, had studied law, served as an NCO in the Russian army and despised the Bolsheviks for the way they treated his family. He was a sportsman; he was a boxer and he played football as a central defender for Russia in the 1912 Stockholm Olympics. He also played for the *St Petersburg Unitas*, the national champions. He suggested to Agar a small cove at Terrioki, about 3 miles from the border, which had once been the home of the Imperial Yacht Club but was now deserted. Terrioki village and garrison were a couple of miles away inland away from the yacht harbour and had a railway line to Helsingfors.

The cove was well-suited for their needs, being 25 miles from Petrograd and 30 miles from the Royal Navy's forward base at Biorko Sound. Gus developed a rapport with Peter, who, as a courier, pointed out that there were several passages through the breakwaters between the northern fortresses. Gus asked Peter if he could find a smuggler who could act as a pilot to find a way through the breakwaters, and his courier found one – Veroline.

Gus Agar gave a lecture at the Royal United Service Institution on 15 February 1928, in which he mentioned his courier service.

He intended to cross the line of forts in one of my boats shortly after midnight at slow speed: once through, to push on at full speed to the mouth of the Neva, when speed would be reduced again until we arrived at a pre-arranged spot. We carried a small rowing 'pram' on board, which we launched and either brought off an agent or took one ashore. The return journey was managed early in the morning, usually at daylight under the Red Flag and a special pendant only flown by Commissars. After passing the forts, our course was shaped towards the Tolboukin Lighthouse to divert suspicion, and, when out of sight, again north and back to base. In all, thirteen trips were made and only twice were we challenged and came under fire.

At 7.30 pm, dressed in an ill-fitting brown suit, Gus approached the meeting with some alarm. Walter Cowan was a short, fiery individual, known as 'Titch', but who got along surprisingly well with Gus Agar. Unfortunately, this did not extend to his fellow sailors. In March 1921, he took command of HMS *Hood*, which was not the happiest period as a general strike had been called. Two months later, *Hood* was at Rosyth where her crew were to protect essential services. As there was disruption in the coal mines and public transport, it was discovered that some of the seamen's messes were decorated with red bunting, which Cowan took as an incitement to mutiny. The master-at-arms was sentenced to three years of penal servitude while other seamen had lesser sentences – it did not make for a happy ship.

Agar explained his orders to Cowan. They were close to the border to transport the couriers in and out of Petrograd and they would have to silently pass through the forts to the north of Kotlin Island to pick up or drop the messengers at the northern outlying islands. He revealed the news that Peter Sokolov had told him of the gaps in the breakwaters through which the smugglers could navigate. Some of the breakwaters were incomplete between the forts, and with the guidance of a smuggler, they were able to creep through. This was something the Finnish smugglers knew about, but the Bolsheviks would not be expecting. It may have been the duplicity of the contractors to have left gaps between some of the forts, thus allowing the CMBs to pass easily through them. Cowan was particularly interested in the CMBs being able to skim over the Russian minefields. Agar half-joked at the possibility of raiding Kronstadt harbour, and Cowan responded by saying that if Agar had indeed attacked it, he would have recommended him for the Victoria Cross. The CMBs had nothing greater than small arms to defend themselves with. Prophetically this turned out to be true and Agar also asked Cowan for two torpedoes to destroy the two battleships in Kronstadt. He put it in a way that would appeal to his commander, who was himself bent on sinking the leviathans. Dukes pointed out that 'C' had given him permission to engage the enemy wearing naval uniforms and flying the White Ensign.

> I had been told to avoid all operations which could involve us in a hostile act, as our boats were supposed to be civilian in character, yet these torpedoes might come in very useful in self-defence if we found ourselves up against Russian ships.

Returning to his hotel, Gus woke up the next morning to catch a train to Turku (Abo in Swedish) to make preparations for the arrival of his two CMBs with Ed Sindall and the two mechanics, Piper and Pegler. Gus' team had all booked into the Grand Hotel in the city centre and it was noted that the meals were 'at ruinous prices'. The recently-independent country was neither pro-British nor pro-Bolshevik, but during the war had been pro-German. The British were at pains to cultivate good relations with Finland, who went to great lengths not to antagonise its powerful neighbour, Russia. The following day, HMS *Voyager* arrived to tow the CMBs to Biorko Sound. Sadly, the tow was a disaster and the engines in two boats were swamped by the choppy water. Reaching Biorko Sound, they exercised the boats but only managed to reach speeds of 20mph. *CMB-4* had the worst damage following an explosion, grinding metal and the big ends seized. The SS *Francol* was a recently-built steam tanker which had a crew of mechanics who knew how to put an aircraft engine together. It took two days to remove the old engine from *CMB-4* and winch it aboard the *Francol*. On the evening of 10 June 1919, HMS *Versatile* arrived with a new Fiat engine which was fitted to *CMB-4* by Beeley and Hampsheir.

By 11 June, the two men had been working for three days to install the new engine and make sure the rest of the complex parts were working. Hampsheir was standing by to help Beeley, who was working on a difficult pipe. Calling out to Hampsheir to assist, Beeley received no response. Crawling out of the cramped engine room, Beeley could not see his helper. He then glanced into the water between the *Francol* and *CMB-4* and saw bubbles rising to the surface. Jumping in to the freezing water, Beeley surfaced to find the swell had pushed

*CMB-4* close to the tanker. He felt something strike his foot and he reached down and grabbed the collar of Hampsheir's boiler suit. Unable to move Hampsheir, several hands, including Sindall and Piper, managed to haul the unconscious officer onto *CMB-4*. A session of life-saving techniques produced a fit of coughing and in a short time Hampsheir was revived. Hampsheir's version was somewhat different. He was a highly-strung person who suffered a terrible shock when his older brother, who worked as a Company Quartermaster Sergeant for the Royal Engineers, died just thirteen days after the Armistice. John Hampsheir was in a badly shaken state and dealt with his brother's death in a personal way. It is not known if Hampsheir attempted suicide or just happened to fall overboard. Either way, he rested while Marshall and Piper took over.

Cumming had given permission to keep their uniforms and a small White Ensign hidden aboard each boat. Gus promised that they would dress in naval uniform, fly the White Ensign and attack the Russians if they attacke them first. Cowan did not dismiss the request but said that he would give some thought to the idea. The *Vanessa* took Gus and Scale back to Helsingfors, but by that time the mission was not in any way secret. Agar asked the agent, Raleigh Le May, to get hold of a letter from the Finnish Minister of the Interior exempting the CMBs from Customs searches. Furnished with the permission of the Finnish authorities, they were able to use the disused Imperial Yacht Club, where it would be possible to maintain and run their CMBs in and out of Petrograd. The skimmers, although extremely fast, were delicate vessels made of wood, which gave them lightness. They were dependant on aero engines, which were apt to malfunction, and chose to alternatively use the two CMBs to run between the fortresses on the north side of Kronstadt as these were nearer to the Russian coast.

Peter Sokolov had also received information about the fortress at Krasnaya Gorka (Little Red Hill), which guarded the southern shore at Estonia. On 12 June the garrison revolted and for four days hoisted the white flag in the hopes that the White Russians and British would come and rescue them. This did not happen, and they were powerless to defend themselves with the Bolshevik artillery pointing west and north. The Bolshevik navy used its battleships to bombard the fortress from the rear and reduce it to rubble. The White Army's failure to relieve or advance on the fortress was something for which the Estonians never forgave the White Russians and the Bolsheviks.

While Gus was at Biorko, he received a telegram from an agent named Broadbent to hurry at all costs to Terrioki. Wondering about the urgency, he immediately set off in *CMB-7*, cramming in Sindall, Marshall, Beeley, Peter Sokolov, Hall and himself. There were no villages or houses along the thickly-forested shores and Gus took the precaution of staying well out to sea in case any Finnish guards attempted a potshot at them. With six people on the CMB, they were overloaded but were able to make into the yacht basin. The flashing signal helped guide them in, and leaving Peter on the craft, they tramped through the woods to Broadbent's house. The urgent message which Broadbent sent was of no importance and Gus was annoyed to have been dragged from Biorko in an overloaded boat for little reason.

Gus had rented the 'Villa Sakharov' near the yacht basin for the outrageous sum of 3,600 marks per month. During their stay, they were visited by a variety of Russian refugees, who were billeted in neighbouring villas. For a secret mission, their cover was blown. They attempted to keep very quiet as to why they were so close to the border but they confessed that they were an advanced post for Admiral Cowan's forces.

The local smuggler named Veroline agreed to act as a pilot but his services did not come cheap. Gus had to hand over £25 with a proviso of a further £50 if they got back safely. On 13 June they approached the line of forts which were only 15 miles from Terrioki by a wide curving route. Moving at 20 knots, *CMB-7* throttled back until they were moving at a quiet 8 knots and slowly approached the gap between the 6th and 7th forts, where there was a passage through the breakwater. Veroline had travelled this route before and was confident they would not get entangled by the breakwater. The forts were silent and dark, and they passed through without any danger. Once free of the fortresses, they opened up and sped at 36 knots towards the northern side of Petrograd. It took them half an hour to reach their destination and they stopped about 500m from where they were to drop their courier. Peter climbed into his skiff before paddling ashore. Hiding the skiff in the reeds, he flashed a signal to Gus, who headed back to Terrioki. Now Peter had to walk into Petrograd to find 'ST25'.

Gregori Rasputin.

Lenin, Trotsky and Lev Kamenov.

Alexander Kerensky.

Sir Mansfield Cumming.

Paul Dukes.

Dukes disguised as Joseph Afirenko.

Alexander Maskovich.

Alexander Bankau.

Paul Dukes and his Cheka pass.

Lieutenant Augustus Agar.

Terrioki Yacht Club.

John Hampsheir looking shell-shocked with Gus Agar in slippers and Hugh Beeley looking smug after the sinking of the *Oleg*.

Richard Marshall.

С. Петербургъ
St.- Pétersbourg

Великобританское посольство
Ambassade d'Angleterre.

www.nevsky-prospekt.com

British Embassy in Petrograd.

Sinking of the *Oleg*.

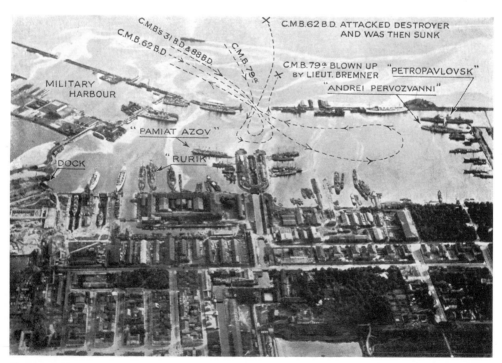

C.M.B.s 31 B.D.
C.M.B. 62 B.D.
C.M.B. 79ᵈ
C.M.B. 62 B.D. ATTACKED DESTROYER AND WAS THEN SUNK
C.M.B. 79ᵈ BLOWN UP BY LIEUT. BREMNER
"PETROPAVLOVSK"
"ANDREI PERVOZVANNI"
MILITARY HARBOUR
"PAMIAT AZOV"
"RURIK"
DOCK

Kronstadt Harbour.

*Pamiat Azova.*

*Andrei Pervozvanny.*

*Petropavlovsk.*

Peter Sokolov.

The 55 foot CMBs at Biorko. One
CMB has a VC on its steering bridge.

A. Gefter.

Lieutenant Gordon Steele with his Victoria
Cross.

Commander "Tommy" Dobson on his wedding day. On his left is Alexander Graham Bell.

Gus Agar saluting the CMB4 as it passed through Alton.

On the return journey, Gus had another idea. Threading their way through the gap between forts 6 and 7, they headed for the Tolbukhin lighthouse from where they could have a good view of the water to the rear of Krasnaya Gorka. He could distinguish two large warships, the *Petropavlosk* and *Andrei Pervozvanni,* with a number of shielding destroyers, standing to the rear of the fortress ready to open fire. Although he was in charge, when Gus decided to torpedo one of the battleships, the rest of the crew were astonished. Dressing into their naval uniforms and hoisting the White Ensign, they prepared to attack one of the Bolshevik warships. As they moved off, there was a grinding sound and the boat came to a standstill. Now any attack was off the menu. Beeley reported that the engine had stripped a gear but he somehow managed to ease the CMB into a few knots which would take them back to Terrioki.

One incident that occurred on 14 June was observed by Gus through his telescope when he ascended the Russian church. He spotted a small Russian gunboat, the *Kitoboi,* approach the submarine HMS *L-12,* which was on patrol in the area. Captain Blacklock launched a boat and sent an officer to find out what they wanted. It seemed that the crew had mutinied and forced the captain at gunpoint to surrender to the Royal Navy. The submarine escorted the Russian gunboat out of the area and it was turned over to a destroyer. *Kitoboi* was sent to Biorko where she was used as a fleet tender, transporting stores to the seaplane base.

With *CMB-7* out of commission, Agar was forced to go to Biorko and try and retrieve *CMB-4*. After a terrifying journey though the forests in an old Benz saloon – in which he helped the driver chop and remove fallen trees from the dirt track – he arrived and told Hampsheir that they should return the following day. With *CMB-4* ready, Gus took along with him a couple of seamen, Turner and Young, nicknamed 'Lenin' and 'Trotsky', to perform routine duties around the villa and to guard the boats. At about 3.00 pm, Gus, Hampsheir, Piper and the two ratings left Biorko and travelled nearer to the shore than previously. When they passed Ino Point, they were greeted with a heavy machine-gun and rifle fire from Fort Ino, which pinged off the metalwork, causing them to alter their direction away from the shoreline. They arrived at Terrioki about 6.00 pm and Gus managed a quick dinner before he picked up Veroline and they set off at 10.00 pm. *CMB-4*, containing Sindall, Hampsheir, Beeley, Peter and Veroline, approached the forts, which were 500m apart. The smuggler pilot directed the boat as they aimed for the middle of the gap between forts Nos. 3 and 4. They could see the barrels of the guns quite clearly and crossed fingers that they did not open fire. The engine was just ticking over when suddenly the guns on the forts opened fire. They had to abort passing through the forts and turned around but were slowed down by the skiff. Peter called for the boat to slow down so he could cut the rope. As he fumbled with his clasp-knife, Hampsheir wielded an axe and cut the rope, setting the skiff free. The guns on the forts had them in range but a sudden boost of power accelerated the CMB away from them. Once clear, Sindall saw Hampsheir curled up behind the cockpit, tended to by Peter. When they got back to Terrioki, Sindall told Gus of Hampsheir's condition and he was taken to a Helsingfors clinic.

Later, *CMB-4* was set to take Peter through the fortresses. He was dressed in his old army uniform and had pinned red stars to his cap and jacket. He also carried a revolver in case he had a confrontation with the Cheka. He had a leather satchel, which was carried by most soldiers, and hidden in his sandwiches were the slips of tissue paper with the latest messages for Dukes. Returning to Terrioki, they waited two more days before setting out for Krestovsky Island in the enemy's territory. The crew of *CMB-4* were on tenterhooks waiting for any sign of Peter and at last they spotted him in his skiff. He was on the brink of exhaustion and had to be revived. Agar decided to return with the Russian Commissar's flag fluttering from the rear of the CMB. Instead of sailing out to Tolbukhin lighthouse to watch the battleships pound Krasnaya Gorka, he decided to return to Terrioki at once. Creeping back through the forts, the crew made certain they did not disturb the enemy, who were either on the island or fast asleep in the fortresses.

Dukes had arranged to meet Peter in a secluded spot in the Winter Palace gardens on 14 June. Hiding behind some bushes, Dukes examined the man in army khaki and saw that it was Peter Petrovich. The surprised Peter was taken aback by the appearance of Dukes disguised as an old man in shabby clothes with a deathly white pallor and shrunken eyes. Dukes went ahead and led Peter to a quiet spot in the garden. They found a stone bench and Peter talked about Gus Agar and his incredibly fast boat which had passed between the forts and deposited him close to Petrograd. Dukes, being short of money, Peter handed him a thick package, which he eagerly secreted in his grubby leather jacket. The courier told him that he was leaving the next day from Krestovsky Island in the north of Petrograd. With Agar's fast CMB waiting, Peter would not appear again until late July or early August.

The following day they met up again at the Winter Palace gardens, where Dukes passed his intelligence to Peter, which was mostly about conditions in Petrograd, and told him that he would not be leaving the city for another month until the twilight White Nights were over. Peter had an appointment with Agar in the early hours of the morning and left the city for Krestovsky Island. He had not realised how well guarded the shoreline was and had to skirt around roadblocks that had been set up by the Cheka. He eventually crept through the reeds and had to lie half in the water until the CMB arrived.

The CMB eventually arrived but there was another hour before it became light. Gus said they should wait for another twenty minutes. Hampsheir flashed a signal which Peter saw. Because of the freezing temperature, he had difficulty in manipulating his own torch but eventually flashed a signal in return. Creeping slowly towards the shore, *CMB-4* spotted the skiff with Peter on the point of exhaustion. Dragging the courier onto the boat, they gave him a tot of rum and he told them that he had made contact with 'ST25', collected the intelligence but that Dukes was not coming.

# Chapter Nine

# The Sinking of the *Oleg*

With his spies being expelled from the embassies in Petrograd and Moscow, Cumming was left with only one agent who could deliver what intelligence he could find. Fortunately, Paul Dukes was able to change his appearance enough times so that the Bolsheviks did not recognise him. He had run out of safe houses and spent four nights in an old, broken-down mausoleum belonging to the long-dead Old Believer, Michael Samashko, in the overgrown Volkovo Cemetery on the south side of the city. Being summer, he was plagued with mosquitoes and had trouble getting any sleep. With the agony of his frostbitten feet, the cemetery was a long walk from the centre of Petrograd. In the space of ten months, he used twenty different disguises. He reminisced in his book, *The Story of 'ST25'*:

> I lay at full length, my head at the open end of the tomb, recalling the events of the day. I was happy. Klachonka was safe – that she would get off I never doubted. Peter, brave Peter, was at that moment hidden in the reeds waiting for his skiff, munching sandwiches Klachonka had prepared, and pulling at his little whiskey flask. Sonia, poor Sonia, was still in prison, but with faith – and ingenuity – surely a way to free her would be found? And who, I ask you, could have been gifted with greater ingenuity than my dear friends, who were far more to me than mere collaborators or conspirators? I pondered and wondered much, while the long light hours of the evening faded imperceptibly into a sweet and gentle dusk. I thought no more of the gruesome bones of Michael Samashko outstretched a foot or two beneath me.

During this period, he managed to gather useful intelligence, including a document from a draughtsman at a factory on the outskirts of the city. He had changed from an old man into a younger man named Alexander Bankau, a draughtsman. This was one of his many disguises and he was able to present himself as Peter's friend at his student lodging house and get at least one night's sleep. There was a hiatus after this, while agent/courier activity was put on hold until the beginning of August. Dukes had learned that there was a counter-revolutionary plot in Petrograd, designed to synchronise with the mutiny in the fortress at Krasnaya Gorka. On 10 June, the garrison revolted against its communist commander; the red flag was removed and a White Russian flag hoisted. In fact, it was not the Russians who garrisoned the fort but the Ingrians, who occupied the northern part of Estonia and craved independence. From his vantage point on the church steeple, Agar saw the battleships *Petropavlovsk* and *Andrei Pervozvanni* towed out of Kronstadt harbour and began bombarding Krasnaya Gorka from the rear. The artillery within Krasnaya Gorka was a land-based fortress with its artillery pointing north and west, and was powerless against the 12in guns of the battleships in the rear.

Two nights later, Agar's crew made one final trip to Petrograd and realised that this could be the last of thirteen trips that had been made through the string of forts. The fort's searchlights were on and Veroline directed the CMB to creep quietly between forts Nos.8 and 9. The Russian men in the forts aimed their beams and were sweeping the area. For some reason the CMB was not detected and made for the north side of Petrograd. The next day, Agar briefed Commandant Sarin, pointing out that both CMBs were out of action due to the White Nights. On the night of 15 July, *CMB-4* and *CMB-7* made for the destroyer's ring around the *Oleg*. Rounding the Tolbukhin lighthouse, *CMB-7* struck a submerged obstacle which broke the propeller shaft. Marshal, although a non-swimmer, dived overboard to find what had caused the problem; it was either a loose mine or some flotsam. When they returned to the small harbour, Piper stripped and examined the shaft. His face told Agar the bad news. The shaft was beyond repair, and with no spares at Terrioki, the attack had to be postponed until the following night.

With the focus on the bombardment of Krasnaya Gorka, any attack from the north was put on hold. The next morning the CMB crews moved to a new house called 'Villa Sakharov', which was closer to the harbour and where they could keep a watch over the boats. The next evening, Gus passed through the forts and made for north of Petrograd, bringing a courier along. Agar had a meal and checked everything. Complete with the torpedo in the rear slot, Agar skippered *CMB-4* and went in search of the *Oleg*. Without *CMB-7*, he was on his own. He received telegrams from Mansfield Cumming about the bombardment of Krasnaya Gorka. 'Boats to be used for Intelligence purposes only. Take no action unless specially directed by S.N.O. (Senior Naval Officer) Baltic.'

Another telegram arrived that evening stating that, 'Admiralty does not approve of any further boats being sent. You must do the best you can with the material at your disposal. Boats should not be used for any other but intelligence work.'

Without contacting John Scale in Stockholm, Agar took it to mean he could go ahead with the attack as there was no time to seek Cowan's endorsement. Agar later wrote: 'I was quite certain in my mind what his (Cowan's) wishes would be and decided to attack the Red ships that very night.'

*CMB-4* had a single torpedo sitting in the trough to the rear of the coastal boat, ready to attack the battleships. It was hit and miss whether a torpedo like this would penetrate the destroyer ring. Agar had gone to the church steeple and saw the two battleships withdraw to Kronstadt harbour as they had used all their ammunition. They were replaced by the *Oleg* and that afternoon the heavy cruiser began its bombardment on the defenceless fortress. On Monday, 16 June, Agar left Terrioki at 10.15 pm, bound for the cruiser. The crew had their naval uniforms with them, and with the skimmer flying the White Ensign, they set off. Gus Agar later wrote about his attack on 17 June 1919.

As on the previous evening, Hampsheir, Beeley and I waited in our CMB in the shelter of the harbour until just before midnight, when, once more, we set out and headed for the Tolbuhin lighthouse. This time we were alone and the object of our attack was the cruiser *Oleg*. Arriving off the lighthouse, we could clearly see the destroyer screen ahead of us. It was necessary to pass through it in order to reach a position from which we could fire our torpedo at the cruiser. I slowed down to minimise the risk of noise and spray which, with a strong wind ahead of us and a high speed, was being thrown up over our heads. We were now creeping through the destroyers in precisely the same way as we crept through the forts on our way to Petrograd, and all seemed to be going well, when I suddenly felt the whole boat quiver and shake. I thought we had hit something and stopped.

Hampsheir appeared from below the hatch with an agonised look on his face. 'The charge has fired, sir', he said.

The destroyers were some 200–300 yards away as *CMB-4* found a breakwater to enable them to make repairs and for twenty minutes they were masked by the darkness within the ring of destroyers.

> I must explain here that we had ingenious device for firing the torpedo by ejecting it from the stern with a hydraulic rammer. The impulse by means of which this rammer was propelled was supplied by firing a small cordite cartridge in a cylinder, which created a pressure against the head of the rammer. Somehow or other, in loading the cartridge, Hampsheir had accidentally fired it. And it was this that caused the shock they felt.

Harry Fergusson explained this operation in his book, *Operation Kronstadt*, and how things had gone awry.

> If the ram would still fire then there was a spare charge in the boat which was kept in case the original cartridge became soaked and refused to fire. But replacing it would be a tricky job and they could both see that Hampsheir was badly shaken. Also the boat was pitching heavily in the rough seas.

Beeley shoved the stricken Hampsheir aside and delicately extracted the smouldering charge and replaced it with a new one. It took less than ten minutes. Finally, Beeley gave the thumbs-up and Agar slammed in the clutch and aimed for his target.

> Keeping low in the darkness of the cockpit, Beeley could not see what had happened to make the charge fire, but he could guess. The safety pin in the cartridge was no more than small T-shaped piece of metal. In order to help remove it, the pin was usually attached to a length of brightly coloured lanyard. But if whoever was priming the charge yanked too hard on that lanyard it was apt to come away in their hand, leaving the pin in the charge. Feeling around on the floor of the cockpit compartment, Beeley found a pair of pliers. He guessed that Hampsheir must have accidentally pulled the lanyard off and had then tried to remove the tiny pin using the pliers … When Hampsheir had succeeded he must have given a hard tug and

somehow struck the lever which set the cartridge off. They were lucky that they had not all been killed.

Agar continued his account.

> Fortunately, in addition to these mechanical arrangements, there also fitted in the boat two stout iron stops operated by a lever near the steering wheel, which held the torpedo in the boat, irrespective of the rammer, provided the stops were down. Fortunately, I placed this lever in the "down" position so that when the cartridge prematurely fired, the only result was a severe concussion to the hull of the boat and a tremendous shock to Hampsheir, who must have injured his hand.

The concussion was severe enough to shatter the unfortunate Hampsheir's nerves. The CMB began to ship water and progress was reduced to a crawl. Agar ordered Beeley and Hampsheir to extract the fired cartridge and put in another one – a difficult operation with the boat rolling in the sea. It was dark and their hands were cold. 'Set a new charge', Agar ordered Beeley as he emerged from the engine room. The safety pin in the cartridge was a small T-shaped piece of metal attached to a lanyard. Hampsheir had given it a hard tug, which prevented the two stops from allowing the torpedo from launching and blowing up the CMB. Using a screwdriver, Beeley managed to prise the remains of the cartridge out of the chamber. He was mystified that the stops had held the torpedo against the power of the hydraulic ram. He found a nut that connected a copper tube to the explosion bottle that had worked loose. Using his pliers, Beeley tightened the nut and Hampsheir fetched a new cartridge. Now the boat was ready to complete its attack on the *Oleg*. Agar wrote:

> All through this time of intolerable suspense, my eyes were on the destroyers on either side of us, now distant only two to three hundred yards. Ahead I could dimly see the silhouette of our target, the cruiser *Oleg*, which I was about to attack. We might at any moment be seen, as it was then just before one o'clock in the morning and the first streaks of early dawn were due to appear, Beeley remained wonderfully calm. There was nothing to be said. It was a time for deeds, not words. At last, Hampsheir popped up from the hatch, 'It's all right, sir, we have reloaded.'

With a sigh of relief, at one in the morning I slipped the clutch. Throwing all caution to the winds, I put on full speed and headed straight for the *Oleg*, which was now clearly visible, and in a few moments we were nearly on top of her.

The shocked Hampsheir held a stopwatch to time the run of the torpedo and he managed this well, before collapsing in the cockpit.

I fired my Torpedo less than five hundred yards away, just as the first shot from her guns was fired at us in return. Then I quickly put the helm over, turning a complete circle. And, with the sea now following us, headed back westward towards the same direction from which we had approached.

We looked back to see if our torpedo had hit, and saw a large flash abreast of the cruiser's foremost funnel, followed almost immediately by a huge column of black smoke reaching up to the top of her mast. The torpedo had found its mark.

The *Oleg* lurched to port and sank in twelve minutes, so she could be clearly seen in shallow waters. Hampsheir was very seasick and badly shocked by the incident with the safety pin in the cartridge. He was contrite over the accident but *CMB-4* made up for it by sinking the *Oleg*.

We tried to give three cheers, but could scarcely hear ourselves for the din of the engines. Yet we could hear the whistle of shells overhead, telling us that both the destroyers and forts were firing at us, but in the uncertain light just before early dawn, speed made us a very difficult target to hit.

Shells exploded in the sea around them, soaking the men and their craft, but none struck home. They were headed for Biorko, where the Bolsheviks thought they had come from. After half an hour, they were able to turn for home. Hampsheir's nerves finally gave out and he spent many weeks in a sanatorium before he was invalided back to England. At 3.00 am, out of range from the destroyer screen, they made a large detour towards Biorko Sound, but changed direction and headed north where they reached Terrioki.

We carried on in the direction of Biorko Sound (where the British Fleet were based) as I wanted the forts to think that was where we had come from instead of Terrioki, and we did not turn round to the northward until we were out of sight of them.

On 24 June 1919, Gus Agar sent a message to the Admiralty, in which he laid out his mission to sink the *Oleg*:

The next night, Tuesday, 17 June, I again set out in my one remaining boat to make an attack. Left harbour at 10.30 pm in CMB No.4 with the following crew on board besides myself: Acting Sub-Lieutenant John White Hampsheir, RNR, Chief Motor Mechanic Hugh Beeley RNVR, Official Number M.B.2108. Proceeded to round Tolbuhin Light House which I passed three miles to the Westward when of here the wind got up and there was a considerable sea for our small craft.

From there I ran due south until within a mile of the Southern shore, in order that should I be observed, the enemy might think the attack was made from either from Krasnaya Gorka, which was then in the hands of the 'Whites' or from Biorko Sound. From this position I steered East by North and made for Kronstadt Roads.

On entering the Roads and when about four miles South East of Tolbouhin Light House, I observed a large enemy cruiser, which I recognised as the *Oleg*, at anchor. She was guarded by four destroyers, one Patrol Gunboat or Sloop and one Torpedo Boat ... Course was shaped to pass between the Destroyers and the Torpedo Boat and I gave Sub-Lieutenant Hampsheir orders to remove all safety pins ad prepare to attack. In removing the safety pin of the firing charge, the lanyard broke and the charge fired. Fortunately the side stops were down and the torpedo was in consequence not ejected. I then turned away, eased down to dead slow speed and prepared another firing charge. This was extremely difficult operation on account of the sea running, and the motion on the boat added to which we were very close to the patrol craft and Destroyers (about 700 or 800 yards). In 15 to 20 minutes we had everything ready again and I would like to mention here the coolness with which Sub Lieutenant Hampsheir helped during this trying time.

I increased speed, passed between the Destroyers and Torpedo Boat, and made for the *Oleg* at full speed. I fired the torpedo when about 800 yards of her port beam (she was heading due west at the time), and turned 16 points to starboard. Torpedo hit just abaft her foremost funnel throwing up a high column of water and some black smoke. Either this gave the alarm or else we were observed as fire was directly open on us from all quarters, though it was difficult under the conditions to see exactly from where.

I steered west and passed between two Destroyers at full speed, who also opened fire. Most of the firing was wild and very erratic but three shots (fire apparently from the forts and appeared to be large calibre about 8 inch) were well directed and fell between 15 and 20 yards over, one just by our stern, momentarily throwing up and straining the engine so I eased down to 800 revolutions and took an observation of the *Oleg*. She appeared then to be underway, as large columns of smoke were coming from her funnels.

The torpedo was fired at 0005 (Finnish Time) and all firing ceased shortly after we eased down to 800 revolutions at 0030. I continued on a Westerly course until well clear of Tolbuhin then turned to the Northward and when close to the coast turned South South East to Terriokki arriving at our base at 1.45 am.

*CMB-4* sank the *Oleg* with only one torpedo; an armoured cruiser with twelve 6in guns, carrying 576 men and weighing 6,975 tons. It was broad daylight by the time the crew reached their port and *datcha*. Young Marshall took a photo of Gus, Beeley and the shell-shocked Hampsheir. This showed Gus Agar wearing carpet slippers, a navy cap and a big smile, Beeley with his crossed arms, looking pleased with himself – while poor Hampsheir was in a state of shock from which he never recovered. Marshall, who had been watching events through his binoculars from the church tower, saw the flash and the column of black smoke as the torpedo struck. The crew at Terrioki were ecstatic and the crew of *CMB-4* were welcomed with huge congratulations. At 3.30 am, after hours of tension, the exhausted crew slept like a log.

Once roused, Agar had to report to the commander of Fort Ino, which was the strongest fortification on the Finnish side. The Russians had constructed it but now wanted it demolished, which was eventually done in 1921 by the Finns. Agar explained to the commander that he had been responsible for the sinking of the *Oleg* and had no alternative but to come clean and explain that the CMB only carried one torpedo. The commandant also pointed to the civilian clothes that Gus was wearing. Gus pointed out that his crew had changed into naval uniform and flown the White Ensign. He pleaded with the commandant to keep secret the Royal Navy's mission.

> But our activities have not ceased and there may be other opportunities of repeating this venture. So will you please do everything in your power to help us keep our secret?

The commandant loaned Agar a car that would take him to the village of Koivisto. Here he borrowed a horse and braved the thick pine forest to reach Biorko Sound. He had to wait until midnight when Cowan arrived on his flagship. Rowing across to meet the admiral, Agar was received by Cowan in his cabin and the admiral was delighted at the result and said, 'This allows me to show them that I have a sting which I can use if they show their noses out of Kronstadt.'

Cowan wrote to all his commanders that the Bolshevik cruiser had been sunk but urged that they did not reveal the CMB had been responsible. The first incident to attract public attention was the report coming through Finland that Russian battle cruiser *Oleg* had been sunk. The Bosheviks had first reported that she had been mined, and later reports alleged that she had been torpedoed by a submarine. It was not for some time that it was generally known that she had been attacked by Lieutenant Agar and his crew on *CMB-4* without any support from other vessels.

Two days later, while he was in the Biorko area, he paid a visit to the Finnish airfield, where he was able to fly with a Swedish pilot named Arthur Reichel, who had volunteered to fly with Mannerheim's army. They flew over the Tolbukhin Lighthouse and descended over the stricken *Oleg*. Gus wrote that she looked like a large dead whale with some superstructure breaking the surface on the bottom of the sea. His elation turned to dismay as the aircraft then flew over the large bastion of Krasnaya Gorka and – instead of the White Russian flag – saw the red flag of the victorious communists fluttering from the battlements.

The admiral advised Gus to return to Terrioki, pick up his two boats and bring them to Biorko, where they could be repaired by the mechanics. Gus had one more interview with the new commander at Terrioki garrison. His name was Sarin; he was a former Russian army officer who had taken over from the pro-German commandant. Sarin cautioned Agar about staying at the abandoned yacht basin and told him that he should take both CMBs to Biorko. Although Sarin had been put in charge of the garrison by the Bolsheviks, he nevertheless still favoured Agar's courier runs to Petrograd.

On 19 June Agar towed the *CMB-7* – with its wrecked propeller shaft – to Biorko Sound. He and his crew were touched when Admiral Cowan ordered his sailors to form up his fleet into two lines and cheer them in. Cowan recommended Agar for the Victoria Cross, which was published in *The London Gazette* on 22 August 1919 and he also promoted him to lieutenant commander on 30 June 1919. The announcement was short and did not describe the enemy or the action.

> In recognition of his conspicuous gallantry, coolness and skill under extremely difficult conditions in action.

In the British Parliament questions were raised but they were easily dealt with. The Secretary of State for Foreign Affairs, Lord Curzon, asked Walter Long, the Secretary of State for the Admiralty 'if he was in a position to give any particulars as to the sinking of the Bolshevik's cruiser'. Long replied that 'the Bolshevik's cruiser, *Oleg*, was sunk by British naval forces which encountered her when patrolling. It was obviously undesirable to give the exact means by which this was accomplished.' Parliament debated for a while but the matter was soon forgotten.

Because of his secret role in ferrying couriers to Petrograd through the forts and sinking the *Oleg*, Agar was engaged in an unofficial presence, and his award was regarded as 'the mystery VC'. Chief Motor Mechanic Hugh Beely RNVR was recognised with the award of the CGM (Conspicuous Gallantry Medal) with the same citation as Agar, with an additional recognition of 'his management of the engine of an obsolete type of motor boat which failed during a previous attempt'. Agar's friend and colleague John Hampsheir received the DSC (Distinguished Service Cross), although he was still suffering from nerves and the shock of the death of his brother a few days after the Armistice. He was later sent to a hospital in Helsingfors and then to Osborne House in the Isle of Wight to recuperate.

The White Nights period meant that the courier trips were suspended. Instead, Agar offered his service to the small force of Ingrians who were in Finland and itching to go to battle with the Bolsheviks. On 26 July Agar took *CMB-4* along the coast to support the Ingrians who were further away in the north. The trenches guarding the Russian border ran down to the coast, to which Agar was able to give covering fire. Unfortunately, his efforts were in vain. The Ingrians did manage to take back some Russian land but to little purpose, as the White general, Nikolai Yudenich, did not follow up and the Bolsheviks recaptured what they had lost.

With the Armistice declared, Britain and the rest of the world suffered a dreadful strain of influenza known as the Spanish Flu, which saw a worldwide death toll of 70 million. The British Labour Party was agitating against any intervention against the Bolshevik Party while the British government was trying to cope with the virus and was lukewarm about supporting the White Russian leaders. With an end to one of the worst conflicts in living memory, and the pandemic that was sweeping across the world, the British government was at the point of bankruptcy and it did not want to know what was happening in Russia.

# Chapter Ten

# Walter Cowan

Cowan stood 5ft 6in tall, had a short temper and a forceful way of diplomacy. He liked Agar's attitude. Cowan's mission was to keep the sea lanes open for the new republics of Finland, Latvia, Estonia and Lithuania, which were under threat from being overrun by Soviet Russia. In January 1919 Cowan's 1st Light Cruiser Squadron was sent to Reval in Latvia to try and prevent the Bolsheviks reclaiming the Baltic States.

Walter Henry Cowan was born in Crickhowell in Wales on 11 June 1871. His father was an officer in the Royal Welch Fusiliers, but for some reason he entered his son into the Royal Navy. Cowan's first active service was in Benin in West Africa in 1895 and a year later he took part in the Mwele Expedition in East Africa. In 1897 he added a clasp to his West African medal in the capture of the 'horror city' by the landing party of 1200 sailors and marines. He was part of the punitive expedition in response to the ambush of a previous British party under Acting Consul General James Phillips. Sir Harry Rawson's troops captured and sacked Benin City, bringing an end to the Kingdom of Benin, which was eventually absorbed into Nigeria.

Cowan caught dysentery and was hospitalised for a year. Towards the end of Queen Victoria's reign, he evaded an appointment to the Royal Yacht but he did accept command of destroyer *Boxer*. He had adhered to the commander-in-chief for a transfer to the shallow-draught *Sultan* in time to fight the Dervishes at Omdurman and the Upper Nile in 1898–99. He was also present at the battles of Atbara and Khartoum, where he fought on the gun-boats on the Upper Nile. He later forestalled the French commander's attempt to annex Sudan by commanding the entire Nile gunboat flotilla during the Fashoda incident. For his service he was awarded the Distinguished Service Order. The khalifa's death in September 1899 prompted Cowan to write the following:

It seemed now the fighting was over in the Sudan, that South Africa was the place for me. After the fight in Benin, I had said to an old friend that the next thing to try was to fight the Khalifa, and now I remarked to Jimmy Watson that we must go for Kruger.

Although not a scholar, he moved up the promotion ladder and became a Military ADC to Lord Kitchener in the Boer War and later Naval ADC to Lord Roberts; both military men. He was at Klip Drift, Paardeberg, where Cronje surrendered, and then onto Pretoria. Hearing that the Admiralty had struck him off the Navy List because he had spent more than two and half years with the Army, it was decided that he would not be included in any promotion but this was soon forgotten. He married Catherine Cayley and enjoyed a long hunting honeymoon in Galway. Returning to England in 1901, Cowan was appointed first lieutenant on battleship *Prince George* and six months later was promoted to commander at the early age of 30. He transferred to the old battleship *Resolution* on guard duty at Holyhead and later took command of HMS *Falcon*, a destroyer under the fleet command of Admiral Jacky Fisher. It was on this destroyer that he annoyed the admiral by lassoing the periscope of a British submarine during an exercise. In 1905 he was appointed a member of the Royal Victorian Order, in 1906 he was promoted to captain, and in 1907 transferred to cruiser *Sapphire*. His promotional movements took him to command all destroyers in the Channel Fleet in 1908, and in 1910 he became captain of the new light cruiser *Gloucester*. In 1912 he became chief of staff to Rear Admiral John de Robeck.

Joining pre-dreadnought battleship *Zealandia* in 1913, Cowan suffered from a spate of mutinies. The battleship had problems with her stokers, in that they wanted to wash themselves having filled the bunkers with coal. They much preferred to wash themselves than clean their coaling suits but Cowan did not agree and was at fault when he stopped the stokers from leave and ordered extra drill. He ordered the twelve stokers to be court-martialled and for them to serve two years' imprisonment. The Admiralty had to annul this sentence and free the stokers. Once again, Cowan felt their Lordship's displeasure.

Cowan later transferred to take command of the *Princess Royal*, which took part in the battles of Dogger Bank and Jutland. In the latter action, the ship suffered more than 100 casualties and required to spend six weeks to effect repairs. In June 1917 he was ordered to hoist his pendant on the cruiser *Caledon* as Commodore of the 1st Light Cruiser Squadron. On September 1918 he was promoted to rear admiral and in 1919 he was commanded to take over the 1st Light Cruiser Squadron in the Baltic, with Cowan flying his flag in the cruiser HMS *Curacoa*. Under the command of Rear Admiral Walter Cowan, as replacement for Alexander Sinclair's force, he took command of the squadron, which consisted of *Inconstant, Galatea, Phaeton, Royalist,* together with several destroyers. Instead of keeping his ships at Riga in Latvia, Cowan moved his base to Reval and then across the Gulf to Biorko Sound. Only 30 miles away, he could just about see the Bolshevik ships leave Kronstadt harbour and have some idea of their intentions.

Cowan was faced with an extremely complex problem, as many different groups attempted to take over control of Latvia, whose independence had been agreed at the Treaty of Brest-Litovsk and endorsed by the British Government. On one occasion, he sent Captain the Hon. Matthew Best of the *Royalist* with two destroyers to Libau in Latvia to oversee the distribution of 500 rifles and ammunition. The Allies had negotiated a peace with the Germans, but under the control of Major General Rudiger von der Goltz, they seized the weapons from HMS *Angora* and threw them into the sea, so the Lettish volunteers could not be armed. On the voyage to Libau, Cowan impressed his officers by ordering the fleet to continue to steam at 22 knots despite the thick fog and minefields. Cowan's forceful brand of diplomacy saw the objective of the exercise achieved and he returned to Biorko Sound.

This brought him into contact with Lieutenant Augustus Agar. Hired by the Secret Intelligence Service to run agents into Petrograd and having established good relations with a mere lieutenant, Cowan was partially taken aback for the request for a couple of torpedoes. The messages went back and forth to London until Cowan spotted that Agar's request could be met. He requested Lieutenant Commander Martin Nasmith VC to send two torpedoes from his Submarine Depot Ship HMS *Lucia* to Biorko Sound, where they were fitted to *CMB-4* and *CMB-7*.

The bombardment of Kransnaya Gorka by the battleships *Petropavlovsk* and the *Andrei Pervozvanni* had prompted the two CMBs to take matters into their own hands. Sadly, as they departed to attack these two giant ships, *CMB-7* hit an obstruction and had to be towed back to Terrioki.

The next day it was battle cruiser *Oleg* who pummelled the fortress into submission. Cowan read Agar's report on the sinking of *Oleg*, and realised he could wreak havoc in Kronstadt harbour. The idea of Gus Agar's impromptu attack on the *Oleg* appealed to Admiral Cowan. He named the Kronstadt Raid 'Operation *R.K.*' after his friend Admiral Roger Keyes.

Contacting the Admiralty, he ordered eight CMBs from Osea Island (one went missing on the voyage to the Baltic). The communist battleships posed a threat to the light cruiser and destroyer fleet he had assembled at Biorko Sound. The minefield that lay between them was a barrier which neither side could breach. The Bolshevik pounding of the Krasnaya Gorka fortress on the Estonian shore put Cowan in a dilemma. His heart told him that he should use the heavier CMBs to sink the battleships within Kronstadt harbour, but any retaliation would mean an all-out war between Russia and Britain. Agar's sinking of the *Oleg* gave him the inspiration to call the Admiralty and ask for a flotilla of 55ft, twin-engine CMBs carrying two torpedoes to assemble at Biorko Sound. He discussed the plan with Agar, and the idea of using the bigger CMBs to strike a heavier blow appealed to the Admiral. He knew that the CMBs would easily ride over the minefield and the attack would take the Bolsheviks by surprise. Kronstadt occupied the western half of Kotlin Island, which stood in the middle of the entrance to Petrograd Bay and was seen to be the most heavily-defended naval arsenal in the world. Although the Bolsheviks had removed most of the regular officers and experienced personnel, those who were left created Kronstadt a formidable target. Cowan wrote of the CMB crews from Osea Island;

> Their cool disciplined, daredevil gallantry turned what the outside world would have called a forlorn hope into a legitimate operation which met with far greater success than I had ever hoped.

On 1 January 1920 Walter Cowan sailed away from Copenhagen and his association with the Light Cruiser Squadron came to an end. It took him three days of stormy weather to sail to Plymouth and his flag was hauled down from HMS *Delhi*. On 31 March 1921 he took up command of HMS *Hood*, which was not the happiest period for Cowan due to his short temper and quick judgement. Within two months he found himself at Rosyth, where her crew were ordered to protect the essential services of the general strike. There was already disruption in the mines and transport and the country was already paying the cost of the First World War. Dissatisfaction had spread to the crew's messes when it was found that red bunting bedecked the walls to celebrate Red Russia. Cowan took it to mean an incitement to mutiny and it did not make *Hood* a happy ship.

After two years on the *Hood*, Cowan took a reduction in promotion as commander-in-chief in North America and the West Indies. By 1926 he had been promoted admiral and finished his career as First and Principal ADC to King George V. In 1929 he was placed on the retired list at the age of 59; by this time he had separated from his wife, who subsequently died in 1934. He spent his time riding to hounds with the Warwickshire Hunt and seemed to have accepted retirement. However, with the start of the Second World War, he applied for and was taken on as a staff member of the Naval Control Service Office at Grimsby, where he became bored with the paperwork. He appealed to his old friend Roger Keyes and got the job of Naval Liaison Officer to No. 11 Commando, joining them in 1941. During this period, he was on the *Warspite*, which attacked Bardia and other ports behind the Italian lines. When No. 11 Commando was disbanded, he joined the 18th King Edward's Own Cavalry in the Indian Armoured Corps. On 26 March 1941, he was in action against the *Afrika Corps* at Bir Hakim and was later captured. He wrote to Keyes,

> We were holding an unprepared position with 500 men. They attacked us with many tanks and a whole division, and the first wave went clean through, and everyone near me was either knocked over or captured. I got behind an empty Bren-gun carrier and they missed me. After a lull the second wave came on. I'd got into the carrier. An armoured car stopped about forty yards off, and four men got out and came for me. I let drive at them with my revolver and one dropped in front. The others ran back behind their AC. Then the captain of it shouted and gesticulated that I should put my hands up, but this I could not do, so he fired a burst at me and missed. He again hailed me and got no response, so I fired another burst and again missed. I didn't think he could, as I wasn't trying to take cover – just stood there with my revolver hanging down empty, so he had every chance and was welcome to it. But I felt after missing me twice that was enough, and I got out of the carrier and pointed

to my empty pistol, and walked up and asked what he wanted. He motioned me to get up on to his car, and that was the end, and I grieve that it's all over.

He was taken into captivity, but because of his age, they released him after nine months. He returned and joined the No. 2 Commando unit on 16 January 1944 with Tito's guerrillas on the island of Vis. By 1944 he had to accept he was just too old for the active life and returned to England. In September 1944 he was presented with a bar to his DSO for the action he had been in on the islands of Croatia – Solta, Mljet and Brac. In the final year of the war he went to Holland and took part in the capture of Walcheren. He also crossed the Rhine and was at the surrender of the Germans. His last honour was when he was gazetted Honorary Colonel of the 18th Cavalry and visited his friends at Risalpur on the North West Frontier. During his very active career, he was involved in many raids and eventually died in 1956 at Kineton, Warwickshire, at the age of 85.

# Chapter Eleven

# March 1919

Agar and Dukes' trusted courier was Peter Petrovich, but his surname was Sokolov. He was born on 28 December 1890 in Petrograd and he kept up an association with Paul Dukes which lasted through the Second World War. After the war, the Russians tried to kill him. He reached Sweden, where he retired with the changed name of Peter Sahlin – similarly named after the Commandant of the Terrioki garrison. He lived to a good age and died on 11 May 1971 aged 80 years old. He was one courier who made many trips but was never apprehended. The only exception was in winter, when he took Paul Dukes' despatches and was fired upon from Sestroretsk and had to beat a hasty retreat further onto the ice. Although he was under surveillance in Petrograd, he somehow managed to evade his Cheka followers. Along with Veroline, he knew the way through the breakwaters between some of the fortresses – something he revealed to Gus Agar. The forts were either well-built stone structures with 8in naval guns, or platforms with a few searchlights and machine guns.

Peter headed for his old student flat on Vasily Island, which had belonged to him when he was a law student. He used it when he was asked to take messages to and fro from Petrograd but thankfully his quarters were not raided. He was savvy in that he left objects in certain positions until they were covered with dust. He had arranged to meet Paul Dukes at the gardens of the Winter Palace, where they exchanged messages. When they parted ways, Dukes had to limp to the Volkovo Cemetery with an important package containing money given to him by Peter. When he arrived at the cemetery, he opened the package behind the mausoleum. It turned out to be poorly-printed roubles on thin paper, which Dukes immediately consigned to small bonfire. Peter had made arrangements for Gus to pick him up from the reeds north of the city but the times he had to avoid the patrols exhausted him. Finally, he managed to float the pram towards the CMB, despite the dawn, and they managed to pick up the courier who was on the point of exhaustion.

The Doctor had trouble at his clinic due to the Cheka and he moved to a private apartment on Vasily Island. He left the hospital with his assistants and headed to the east of Petrograd, well away from the Cheka. In the flat was an elderly lady, who Dukes referred to as 'Aunt Natalia', but her real name was Orlov. Dukes met her on his last trip to Petrograd and described her as a *'deeply religious woman'* and looked like a typical German *Hausfrau*, 'small, neat, tidy and plain'. She was about 50 years old and was devoted to her brother, who had been one of the tsar's librarians. He had been shot on Zinoviev's orders along with the rest of the National Centre to avenge the death of Uritsky. She received no food card but did odd jobs of sewing and some kind of secretarial work. She refused any sort of recompese but did allow Dukes to feed her canaries.

After some weeks Dukes went to a concert at the Winter Palace and on the way back called on an ex-general who furnished him with information about the Red Army. He also gave Dukes a paper that Trotsky had taken against the counter-revolutionary General Kolchak, which was of importance for the British who were supporting him. That evening, Aunt Natalia told Dukes that he had some papers he wanted hidden and she wrapped them tightly in a rubber bag and hid them in a tub of washing. Some time later, Dukes accompanied Aunt Natalia along the straight road of Vasily Island to the Smolensk Cemetery, where she had a family sepulchre. Here, Dukes used the tomb as a secret safe. Dukes escaped from Russia and heard that Aunt Natalia had been condemned to death. She had been taken from Shpalernaya Prison by train to Irinovka, where she was executed; she was shot, alongside two other women.

The Doctor urged Dukes to rest for a couple of days as he was almost lame. He did rest in bed until the following day before he asked for a change of clothes and shoes, which the Doctor provided. The shoes were several sizes too big, but with the bandages he managed to walk in them. He was also keen to attend the Founding Congress for the Third Communist International – or Comintern – in which Lenin's presence would be the highlight. Looking like a student, Dukes was wearing glasses and the Doctor's old clothes.

I was now presented the appearance of a clean shaven, short haired, tidy but indigent, ailing and unfed intellectual.

The Doctor was set against Dukes attending the Comintern but contacted Shura Marenko, who gave up his ticket so Dukes could attend. The Congress took place between 2 and 6 March 1919 in a vast auditorium known as the People's Palace. After Trotsky, Zinoviev and Lunacharsky came Lenin. He was a little man in an ill-fitting suit whose manner was devoid of all reaction to his audience. He was cold and calculating, and Dukes found his speech disappointing with its longwinded arguments on the general evils of the capitalist system and the favouring of the communist point of view. Lenin suppressed all strikes, as they came from the Social-Revolutionary Party. A delegation from the Petrograd factories had come to present their demands to Lenin, but they were turned away. When they returned to their factories, they told their workmates that it had been easier to approach Tsar Nicholas than the head of the Soviet Republic. Feeling better, Dukes travelled to Moscow and received regular reports regarding Soviet internal policy and special reports submitted to Trotsky on the state of the Red Army. Instead of staying in Moscow, he learned that Petrograd was to be made the headquarters of the Comintern. He realised that Petrograd was of greater importance as a base for operations and he was very careful of the Comintern's movements, sending reports back to London, warning of the infiltration by the Bolsheviks.

In March, Dukes was supported by Comrade Rykov, a confirmed communist, who played the balalaika. He was accompanied by Dukes on the piano and they played at Communist Party entertainments. Rykov's beliefs were good, and he genuinely believed the Communist Party to be the saviours of the world's proletariat. He liked Dukes for his fondness of music and he would have made an ideal worker in the Salvation Army. He was also an ideal companion when it became necessary to register with the Communist Party, and both men were left alone, having revealed their communist passes. Ironically, Dukes was invited to become one of these agitators and the committee was persuaded to allow him to remain in Petrograd. His friends concocted a story that ran thus;

> That poor fellow, who limps with a stick, is a victim of capitalist maltreatment. When he was still quite young his father was banished from Russia by the Tsarist Government for holding advanced views ... He refused to fight for the capitalists, so the English put him in jail and deported him back to Russia when the Revolution started.

Among the few Brits who remained in Petrograd was George Gibson of the United Shipping Company. Dukes called on him at his apartment, but was rebuffed when Gibson saw a disreputable figure. As he closed the door, Dukes quickly used the password, 'Henry Earles', and so he was invited inside. Dukes told Gibson he was in urgent need of money as the counterfeit money was useless. His host advanced 375,000 roubles and Dukes gave him a receipt in the name of 'Captain McNeal'. Later, the Secret Service was loath to reimburse Gibson the money he had loaned Dukes and it took some years before Gibson was reembursed.

One of Dukes' agents was a lieutenant in the Admiralty called Kolya Orlov, who involved Dukes in one of his raids on one of the People's Warehouses. He was present at Kolya's house as they set off for the attack. There were six men in the team including Shura Marenko, who had provided Dukes with the Markovich passport. One of the team reported that only two officials were at the entrance, while a couple of sentries where on guard duty. Shura Marenko's brother, Serge, was missing, but the gang went ahead with the robbery anyways. They tied up and gagged the officials and sentries, then began emptying the safe, which was full of gold and silver objects. As it transpired, Shura's brother had informed the Cheka. When they arrived, a gunfight broke out with the five robbers hopelessly outnumbered. One by one the robbers were killed – including Kolya Orlov – until only Shura Marenko was left. Expecting to be apprehended, Shura was about to surrender when out of the blue came a figure toting a revolver. Barely having time to catch a glimpse of them, Shura ran through the alleys until he reached the railway, where he managed to climb into a wagon, which took him to Murmansk. He thought he had been rescued by his brother, who had betrayed the gang to the Cheka. In fact, the mystery figure was his wife, Sonia, who was also Kolya Orlov's sister.

She emptied her gun and was arrested and taken to No. 2 Gorohovaya, where she was interrogated for three weeks. She disclosed nothing and was incarcerated in the Deryabinsky Prison on Vasily Island. Taken from the prison to be interrogated, she spotted Shura's brother, Serge, marching out in Chekist uniform. He had been posing under an assumed name and was challenged by Sonia. Serge was filled with remorse at the robbery and imprisoned for the night. By the morning, he had hung himself in his cell. Sonia remained in prison for four months before managing to escape.

Dukes came to rely on women agents, one of whom was Klachonka. She was a nurse and a friend of Lenin but her real name was Nadezhda Ivanovna Petrovskaya. She was nicknamed 'little hack-horse' and this was a convenient ploy for her concealing her identity. She treated Dukes' lameness and his fake epileptic fits. She also hid his intelligence that kept the Cheka at bay. In winter you could crawl into a hoarding and count nearly twenty hours of darkness, but now in June there was nearly twenty hours of full light. Klachonka suggested that Dukes leave Aunt Natalia's flat and stay at the Doctor's apartment for awhile. Two weeks later a search party entered the Doctor's flat and Klachonka said to them:

> Now I have told you, the person on the couch is an invalid, he is subject to fits at the slightest disturbance, and if you make a noise, he may have a fit at any moment.

The search ceased abruptly and Klachonka ushered the Cheka out of the room. She was already under arrest but managed to stay until her assistants arrived. A few weeks later she was taken to Moscow by convoy to have a personal interview with Lenin, who verified his knowledge of her.

Other female agents helped Dukes in various ways as well. Aunt Natalia took him to a church where he hid his reports in the family vault. Vera Alexandrovna, who ran a 'forbidden cafe' Dukes frequented, was arrested. Laura Cade – whom Dukes had known since 1912 – hid his intelligence in books on her shelves. Varia and Stepanovna were both housekeepers; Varia – who was also a nanny – was sending messengers to Finland. They were very good at hiding reports in rather remote places which the Cheka found difficult to find.

Klachonka provided Dukes with a rug and shawl to protect him from the clouds of mosquitoes in the Volkovo Cemetery. Meanwhile the White Army approached within 20 miles southwest of Petrograd, aided by six tanks driven by British soldiers. They were resentful that the British had supported the independence of the Baltic States. Although they looked certain to overwhelm the Bolsheviks with their tanks, the White officers were envious that the tanks were being driven by British servicemen and in a fit of spite, they filled the petrol tanks with sand, which rendered the tanks unusable.

In Paul Dukes' book *Red Dusk and the Morrow,* he related another scheme devised by a friend in a prominent position in Admiralty.

> On a certain day, a tug was to be placed at the disposal of this officer for certain work near Kronstadt. The plan he invented was to tell the captain of the tug that he had been instructed to convey to the shores of Finland a British admiral who had secretly visited Petrograd to confer with the Bolsheviks. At midnight the tug would be alongside the quay. My friend was to fit me out in sailor's uniform and I was to pose as the disguised British admiral. Then, instead of stopping at Kronstadt, we should steam past the fort and escape, under the Soviet flag and using Soviet signals, to Finland.

Unfortunately, two days later Dobson's CMB raid on the harbour put paid to this escape plan.

# Chapter Twelve

# Dobson's Kronstadt Raid

At the Osea Island Base at the mouth of the Blackwater River, a flotilla of nine 55ft CMBs was assembled for the lengthy voyage to the Baltic. Four of these carried two 18in torpedoes, while the remainder carried just one each. They were towed across the North Sea in pairs by the destroyers of the 20th Flotilla. It was a slow and difficult journey of 1,600 miles, as illustrated by Agar's two CMBs. The tow parted on less than sixteen times which caused the boats to be swamped and one CMB was lost.

The flotilla was under the command of Commander Claude 'Tommy' Congreve Dobson, an ex-submariner and a relative newcomer to the CMB. He was popular with the young officers, and according the Gus Agar, he was a tower of strength and was known throughout Osea Island as 'Dobbie.' As Dobson had little experience of handling CMBs, he was given an experienced first officer, Lieutenant Russell 'Beans' McBean, who would be responsible for handling the flotilla leader. Dobson was not alone as there were two other submariners, Lieutenants Archibald 'Mossie' Dayrell-Reed and Gordon Steele.

Before he joined the Osea Island group, Tommy Dobson had been in command of submarine *C27* which left Longhope in the Orkneys on 18 July 1915 to meet trawler *Princess Marie Jose*. A hawser was attached and *C27* remained submerged during daylight hours, coming up to ventilate only after dark. The trawler took her to Fair Isle before steering south-easterly. This was a fortunate course, for it led her straight towards an incoming German submarine whose intention was to pass through the Fair Island Channel. On 20 July Dobson received a message from the skipper on the trawler that a submarine had been spotted about 2,000 yards away. Unable to reply, Dobson waited for five minutes and slipped the tow. Meanwhile, the crew on the trawler simulated panic and the German submarine moved closer. From the submarine *C27*, Dobson fired a torpedo at a range of 500 yards, which went under the stern of the

German *U-23*. He fired a second torpedo, which hit the enemy below the conning tower, sending up a column of smoke and spray. When cleared, the enemy submarine was seen sinking but they managed to rescue the commander, two officers and four seaman and stokers. For this action, he was later awarded a Distinguished Service Order.

Admiral Cowan gave orders to divert attention from the CMBs by using the Royal Naval Air Service fighter aircraft to launch an attack on Kronstadt. On 30 July 1919, ahead of the CMBs and under the command of Major David Donald, nine aircraft took off from *Vindictive*, as the shore-based airfield was not ready. As they were airborne, they saw coloured flares appearing from the forest on their left, which was a warning that Kronstadt was about to be attacked. As they approached in the early hours of the morning, all the forts were on high alert. The anti-aircraft fire was accurate and the obsolete aircraft were forced to fly at 4,000ft, from where they dropped their small bombs. No aircraft were hit but they did start two large fires, causing minimal damage. The air attack made the defenders think that the bombings would come from the air and not from the sea.

In the meantime, Agar and his two crews sat off the Tolbukhin lighthouse to rescue any aircraft that was forced to ditch in the sea. A Soviet patrol boat appeared outside the line of forts and Sindall asked Agar if he could attack it. Gus gave his permission to take one pass before Sindall returned home. The sentries in the lighthouse started firing but Sindall took evasive action and closed on the Russian patrol boat. Ignoring the shellfire, Sindall released his single torpedo but was aware that he had missed the enemy. Heading straight for the patrol boat, the forts stopped firing, as the two craft were within range and they were apprehensive of hitting their own boat. At 400 yards, Sindall turned the boat hard over giving Richard Marshal the satisfaction of seeing his twin-Lewis gun hit the gun crew. The patrol boat had had enough and made for the forts with Sindall in pursuit. The forts then opened fire and Sindall acknowledged that he was not going to destroy the patrol boat and headed for Terrioki harbour.

The poor state of the CMBs during the long voyage gave the engineers just four days to overhaul the engines and one day to rehearse the attack. Most of the crews were junior officers and ratings who had never faced enemy fire before. Before the raid on the Bolsheviks' naval might, a seaplane flew over the harbour with Tommy Dobson and Bill Bremner, who made a note of the where the warships were in the harbour. They saw the naval facilities split into three harbours; to the west were the cargo ships and to the east was the small military harbour containing patrol boats. The centre was the main military harbour in which the Baltic Fleet was moored. The entrance was quite narrow, just 50m across, and outside the entrance was placed a heavy destroyer, the *Gavril*, ready to repulse any enemy ship that tried to enter. Dobson assigned the experienced Lieutenant Laurence Napier to sink the *Gavril* before the second wave went in.

On the afternoon of 15 August, the crews took their one and only rehearsal of the raid. Based on the photographs taken previously, different coloured buoys marked the positions of the primary targets. Although the *Pamiat Azova* could be sunk from the entrance of the harbour, the two battleships caused a greater problem. They were moored on the far-left corner of the harbour, which would be a dilemma for the first wave of experienced crews. *CMB-31* and *CMB-88BD* were called upon to attack the mock battleships and reached 30mph before *CMB-31* crashed into the buoys masquerading as the harbour wall. They then practiced until they managed to release the torpedo and turn sharply, avoiding the hospital ship moored alongside the 30ft thick wall. The six CMBs spent the entire afternoon drilling until most of them had mastered the raid.

With the weather turning the sea choppy and windswept, the attack was postponed until three days later. Finally, at 9.20 pm on 17 August, they started their engines, left *Vindictive* and moved out of Biorko Sound. By midnight on 18 August 1919, the eight CMBs were approaching Kotlin Island. The weather conditions were now ideal for the attack, with a dark night and a flat calm. They proceeded to Inonemi Point at 18 knots but they had lost contact with Lieutenant Agar and two of the following CMBs on the way. As the flotilla approached Kronstadt on the eastern side, two of the CMBs had engine difficulties. Sub-Lieutenant Francis Howard in *CMB-86BD* had a big end seized and he was forced to remain outside the forts. *CMB-72A*, commanded by Sub-Lieutenant Edward Bodley, had his firing gear shot away and was forced to return to Biorko. With just six CMBs and Agar's 40-footer, they were led by Commander Tommy Dobson, who later wrote:

I left the *Vindictive* with eight CMBs and proceeded to a rendezvous off Inonemi Point. Owing to the darkness it was impossible to see how many boats were keeping in company and all signalling was strictly forbidden. I arrived at Inonemi Point ten minutes before the appointed time of leaving, and stopped. The remainder of the flotilla joined up about midnight. I then proceeded towards the North Channel at nineteen knots, Lieutenant Agar proceeding independently according to plan. I passed to southward of Fort No.4 and then between forts No.8 and 10. By this time I was little late on programme time and the air raid had commenced, so I should have liked to have increased speed, but the difficulties of navigation were great that I had to reduce rather that increase.

No sign of Lieutenant Agar (in *CMB7*) and *CMB24* and I could only see two boats following me, Nos.79 and 88. These two boats had kept perfect station the while the whole time. However, the air attack was in full swing, I determined to press on with the boats I had, rather than wait on the off chance of being able to pick up stragglers. I found the Petrograd Canal (Channel) and proceeded up it. Lieutenant Bremner on *CMB79* taking station ahead of me, as arranged. We found a flotilla leader guarding the entrance to the Middle Harbour. But no one on deck; No.79 left her on the starboard hand and turned and entered the basin causing me to stop to avoid confusion at the entrance. No.79 carried out his orders and torpedoed the submarine depot ship. I then entered the basin and Lieutenant McBean succeeded in hitting the *Pervozvanni* with two torpedoes. I then saw No.88, who had followed me into the basin, put one torpedo in the *Andrei Pervozvanni* and one into the *Petropavlova*. Machine gun and rifle fire being very hot at this time; all three boats started to retire and appeared all right. I took the lead, followed by No.88. I think No.79 must have disabled coming through the entrance, and later caught fire and was destroyed.

As we were passing through the south-west corner of the Military Harbour I saw another boat entering. This was apparently No.72 (Sub-Lieutenant Edward Bodley) who had trouble with her steering gear and had later joined up a long way astern of Lieutenant Agar's division. He was unable to enter the basin owing to his steering gear and attempted to torpedo a destroyer who had come to the assistance of the flotilla leader, but his firing gear was shot away. He then retired, and on going through the forts discovered No.86 (Sub-Lieutenant Francis Howard) in trouble and at the very great risk to himself, stood by her and eventually took her in tow.

During the time I was in the basin, Lieutenant Agar and No.24 (Lieutenant Laurence Napier) had entered and torpedoed the flotilla leader (*Gavril*) who caught fire and sank. (Not true, as Napier missed and *Gavril* survived). Lieutenant Napier then disappeared, and from reports it is presumed that he tried to retire through the mouth of the South Channel and was disabled by gun fire, or by fouling either nets or breakwater, and was eventually sunk by gunfire.

Lieutenant Commander Frank Brade in *CMB62BD* had followed Lieutenant Agar and *CMB24* through the forts, and according to the reports from aircraft, must have entered the Middle Harbour and fired his two torpedoes at some target unknown. From the same evidence it was presumed that he was set on fire, and sank inside the Middle Harbour. Reverting to Lieutenant Bremner's boat, No. 79, Lieutenant Bodley reports that he saw a burning mass close to the flotilla leader, which he thought was a CMB, but saw no signs of the crew.

I preceded with No.88 in company through the North Channel forts and passed through the northward of No.4 Fort, being heavily fired at with machine gun and rifle fire and guns of various calibres. When clear of No.4 Fort, I stopped letting No.88 go on and waited to see if any more boats were in the vicinity, and signalled a seaplane who came near me. As soon as it became light, No. 4 Fort opened fire on me again, and I moved further west, and again waited. There was no sign of any boat, and I proceeded to the flagship. Sub–Lieutenant Howard in No.86, owing to engine and steering trouble, had great difficulty in keeping in touch, and on passing through the line of forts both engines gave out. By the efforts of Engineer-Commander Yates and two mechanics they managed to get one engine firing on one block of cylinders. It being hopeless to attempt to enter the harbour under such conditions, he resolutely carried out his orders, and patrolled Petrograd Bay ready to attack any hostile craft who might try to interfere with the retirement. He eventually made his way out at his utmost speed of seven knots, and was eventually picked up buy Lieutenant Bodley and towed back. (It appeared that the Petropavlovsk was seriously damaged.)

Both Tommy Dobson and Gordon Steele received their Victoria Crosses from the king after their sinking of two Russian battleships at Kronstadt. Dobson was awarded the VC on 18 December 1919 and Steele his on 25 February 1920. Both men returned to Osea Island but the fast motor boats had had their day. It was disclosed that Dobson was suffering from vision problems and he was admitted to Chatham Hospital in January 1921 for examination. After an operation, he suffered from gradually deteriorating eyesight.

On 8 May 1920 Tommy sailed with two other naval officers for Canada to attend a demonstration of Alexander Graham Bell's high-speed hydrofoil craft, the *HD-4*, which held the world speed record of 70.86mph. Such speeds were of interest to the Admiralty for the adoption of hydrofoils to the CMB fleet. The Naval Mission watched nine trials between 7 and 31 July and Dobson reported favourably that the hydrofoil would be significantly better than the CMB. While watching the trials, he also noticed Edith 'Polly' MacMechan, who was Dr Bell's secretary. Although he did not purchase the *HD-4*, he did leave with a fiancée. Tommy and Polly were married three months later in Bristol, and in 1923 they produced twin girls. His health deteriorated and he was diagnosed as suffering from neurasthenia, what is now called 'combat fatigue'. By 1935 his eyesight was so bad that he took early retirement. He died at the early age of 55 on 26 June 1940 and is buried at Woodlands Cemetery, Gillingham.

# Chapter Thirteen

# Kronstadt Raid

The CMBs were towed the 1,600 miles by destroyers of the 20th Flotilla and arrived in the last week of July. The mechanics set about drying out the engines and making sure they were in good condition. The dark period was between the 17 and 21 August, which was selected as the best time to raid Kronstadt. Commander Dobson and Squadron Leader Donald confirmed about the timing of the raid, allowing the aircraft to begin their attack just before the CMBs arrived. Admiral Cowan also relied on the mixture of fighter aircraft from HMS *Vindictive* who would drop lighter bombs on the dockyard defences so diverting the Bolsheviks' attention from the CMBs and one did manage to set fire to a building. It was a very daring plan, particularly at night, as the pilots were not adept at bombing in the dark. The main purpose was to keep the Bolsheviks diverted enough from the air while the CMBs managed to creep between the forts and meet up outside the main harbour. The idea of using a heavier blow on the Bolshevik heavy ships in Kronstadt appealed to Walter Cowan.

Kronstadt was the most heavily-defended naval arsenal in the world, although the effectiveness of its defences had been reduced by the removal of most of the tsar's officers and the experienced personnel. At the beginning of the attack on Kronstadt, the Bolsheviks' naval force comprised of two battleships (the dreadnought *Petropavlovsk*, and the pre-dreadnought, *Andrei Pervozvanni*), the heavy cruiser *Oleg* (already sunk) and five destroyers of the Novik class. There were thought to be two to four submarines alongside the *Dvina*, formally the *Pamiat Azova*, and four smaller coal-burning torpedo boats and minesweepers. During the attack, some motor launches were thought to be destroyed by Agar's *CMB-7* in the last torpedo attack. A few weeks later, three Bolshevik destroyers were sunk by Royal Navy mines to the south of Kronstadt.

Meanwhile, back at Koivisto near Biorko Sound, the airmen had flattened out the trees and stumps on the landing strip, which enabled the air crew of Cowan's squadron to take off. Swinging the propellers, the 'stick and string' biplanes had taken off into the night and, flying at 60 knots, they came upon Kronstadt after fifteen minutes. Squadron Leader Grahame Donald was to lead the attack on the harbour while the CMBs gradually assembled outside the Main harbour where most of the Bolsheviks' ships were tied up. At 1.30 am they began their bombing raid, but the bombs weighed little more than 112 lb and ineffective. The aeroplanes dropped their bombs and sometimes had the satisfaction of seeing a detonation followed by a red flame. This done, they continued to hold the enemy's attention by diving down the searchlight beams to divert attention away from the CMBs below. It was daring plan to use the mixed bag of aircraft to keep the defenders' heads down despite the minimal use of the small bombs.

The Coastal Motor Boats and personnel that took part in the raid were:

**First team:**

*CMB-79A* – Lt. William 'Bill' H. Bremer RN (wounded; PoW), Sub-Lt. Thomas Usbourne RN (KIA), Chief Motor Mechanic Henry Dunkley RNVR, Chief Motor Mechanic Francis Stephens (KIA), Able Seaman William Smith RN (KIA). One torpedo.

*CMB-31* – Commander Claude 'Tommy' Dobson RN, Lt. Russell 'Beans' McBean RN, Sub- Lt. John Boldero RN, Chief Motor Mechanic Ernest Yeomans, Huva – Finnish contraband pilot, plus one unnamed personnel. Two torpedoes.

*CMB-88BD* – Lt. Archibald 'Mossy' Dayrell-Reed RN (KIA), Lt. Gordon Steele RN. Sub-Lt. Norman Morley RN, plus two unnamed personnel. Two torpedoes.

**Backup team:**

*CMB-62BD* – Acting Lt. Commander Frank Brade RNR (KIA), Sub-Lt. Hector Maclean RN (KIA), Chief Motor Mechanic Francis Thanther RNVR (KIA), Stoker Petty Officer Samuel McVeigh RN (wounded; PoW), Leading Seaman Sidney Holmes RN (KIA). Two torpedoes.

*CMB-86* – Sub-Lt. Francis Howard RNR, Sub-Lt. R. L. Wight RN, Eng Lt. Commander Francis Yates, plus two unnamed personnel. One torpedo.

*CMB-72* – Sub-Lt. Edward Bodley RNR, Sub-Lt. Ronald Hunter-Blair RN, plus two unnamed personnel. One torpedo.

## The attack on *Gavril.*

*CMB-24A* (sunk) – Lt. Lawrence Napier RN (PoW). Lt. Osman Gidd RN (wounded; PoW), Chief Motor Mechanic Benjamin Reynish RNVR (PoW), Chief Motor Mechanic William Whyte RNVR (PoW), Leading Seaman Herbert Bowles (PoW), Able Seaman Charles Harvey (wounded; PoW). One torpedo.

## The attack on Military harbour.

*CMB-7* – Lt. Augustus Agar RN, Sub-Lt. Edgar Sindall RNR, Midshipman Richard Marshall RNVR, Chief Motor Mechanic Hugh Beeley, Veroline – Finnish contraband pilot. One torpedo.

The eight boats were lost in the advance from Biorko to Kronstadt. Agar led two CMBs to the harbour entrance, including Lieutenant Bremner's *CMB-79A* skimmer. His was the first motor boat to enter Kronstadt harbour and his target was straight ahead; the submarine depot ship, *Pamiat Azova*, was a sitting duck. As he accelerated into the harbour, Bremner fired his torpedo, scoring a hit on her starboard beam and turned hard to port. The single torpedo caused a tremendous explosion, opened a large gap into the hull and the *Pamiat Azova* listed 60 degrees to starboard and quickly filled with water. The harbour being shallow in depth, the ship settled on the mud of the seabed and remained there for five years until salvage operations commenced in 1921 until 1924. She was finally broken up in 1929, one of the rare ships from the 1880s to survive thus far. Having achieved the first hit, Bremner pulled alongside the harbour wall and waited, while Dobson and 'Mossy' Reed entered the harbour and began their attack on the two battleships.

In the meantime, Agar in *CMB-7* arrived at the harbour entrance with Napier's *CMB-24A*. The latter set his sights on the *Gavril* and moved to torpedo her. Unfortunately, another CMB crossed his path and he had to make a wide turn to release his torpedo. Almost at the same time, the *Gavril* opened up with her main guns and brought the CMB to a halt, throwing Napier overboard. Before they could recover, two more shells landed alongside, causing the boat to split in half and tumbling the crew into the water.

In order to torpedo the battleships, *CMB-31*, with the experienced helmsman Russell McBean, had to concentrate on moving out of the way of his torpedoes, which required great skill. The restricted space meant that they had to declutch one engine to reduce speed while manoeuvring in such a confined area. For technical reasons the engines were not fitted with a reversing gear so they could not stop their boats going astern. The most that could be done was to take out the clutch to slow the boat down and make sharp turn to port. Agar's mechanic, Hugh Beeley, had a method which worked successfully. He kept a carpenter's mallet, well weighted with lead, with which he beat the clutch as hard as he could before pulling out the lever and making a sharp move to either port or starboard. The battleships were moored at anchor on the left side of the harbour; a difficult manoeuvre to make as they had to accelerate, fire their torpedoes and quickly move out of the way before they were hit.

With scant communication, Lieutenant Commander Frank Brade, commanding *CMB-62*, arrived late. He accelerated into the harbour and collided with Bremner's boat, which was departing. Brade was followed by *CMB-72* and both were ordered to destroy the dry dock in the bottom right corner of the harbour. Dobson told his commanders to ignore the old cruiser *Rurik*, but he did point out that the very last boat left should use its torpedo to sink the old ship and escape as quickly as possible. The next boats to enter the harbour were *CMB-31BD* and *CMB-88BD*, whose targets were the *Petropavlovsk* and the pre-dreadnought *Andrei Pervozvanni*. These were the plumb ships to be sunk. The Admiralty issued a statement in which they said:

> The Bolshevik warships in Kronstadt Harbour had long constituted
> a formidable threat to our mine-sweeping operations, which were
> being undertaken with the ultimate object of sending foodships to

Kronstadt and Petrograd. It was necessary in order to safeguard our position that this menace should be destroyed as soon as possible. The squadron consisted of the battleships *Petropavlovsk* and *Andrei Pervozvanni*, the cruisers *Oleg* and *Rurik*, three or five submarines, three or four large destroyers and about the same number of torpedo boats. The following details of the action have been received by the admiralty from the Senior Naval Officer in the Baltic, Rear-Admiral Sir Walter Cowan. Rear-Admiral Cowan reports:

'The position of the ships in the harbour had been ascertained by aerial photographs and the attacks on them have been rehearsed by the boats against our ships with water space so limited that the conditions of helm and speed were identical. Aircraft were to co-operate and it was planned that they should arrive and bomb the harbour just before the CMB's engines could be heard. This time-table was most accurately carried out, with the result that the first three coastal motor-boats passed the line of forts and entered the harbour without a shot being fired.

'Each boat had a different objective, embracing the torpedoing of *Petropavlovsk* and *Andrei Pervozvanni*, *Pamiat Azova*, *Rurik*, the patrol vessel guarding the entrance, and the gates of the biggest dock. Of these six enterprises, four were achieved. The boats entrusted with the other two have been accounted for, and it may be that, before being destroyed, as I fear, it may be assumed they are, may have struck some blow, the results of which may become apparent by further photographing. The results were gained not only by dauntless disciplined bravery at the moment of attack, but by strict attention to and rehearsal of every detail beforehand by every member of the personnel, both of boats and also of the Air Force. Of the latter there is this to say: that though all their arrangements for bombing were makeshift, and the aerodrome from which five machines had to rise in the dark was a month before a wilderness of trees and rocks, and in size is quite inadequate, not one of the nine machines (sea and land) failed to keep to its time-table or to lend the utmost and most effective support during and after the attack to the coastal motor-boats.'

Lieutenant Gordon Steele kept a diary of the raid.

Preparations for the raid were rushed through as some of the boats had been damaged during the passage from England; the engines of my boat in particular took a long time to pick up after the soaking they had had. We worked morning, afternoon and evening to get them right; but, even so, on the day before the raid we could only work up to three-quarters of our full speed, and I was afraid this might reduce the speed of the whole flotilla. Final preparations were made on the 17th and 18th August. The plan of the Operation was explained by Commander Dobson to all officers, and a short rehearsal carried out in front of the parent ship *Vindictive*. Finally, an address was given by the Admiral (Cowan) to all concerned. He had taken the greatest personal interest in all our preparations and knew every individual serving in the flotilla.

The officers of the *Vindictive* gave us a good send-off and we were treated as their guests that night for dinner. After dinner we got into our 'glad-rags', i.e. tin hat, Gieve's life-saving waistcoat, sweaters – or just whatever we thought would give us the best chance of this adventure.

It was half moon. The night was cloudy with a calm sea and light wind. 10 p.m. We started up, seven in all, in fine form. Our engines made a great deal of noise at starting, and everyone in Biorko Harbour thought we were certain to wake up the 'Bolshies' before we arrived. My boat ran very well and gave us no trouble. We had on board Dayrell-Reed (Captain), myself, Sub-Lieutenant Morley (who had been midshipman in my division in the *Iron Duke*) and two motor mechanics.

After about ten miles of the distance had been covered, some of the boats were seen dropping a long way to stern. Every now and then we flashed a light in their direction to show them where we were. We stopped off Ino Point for a short time to allow them to pick up. I took the opportunity to pump out our last boat as she was never properly watertight and had to be pumped out every few hours. At Ino, which was the assembly point, we waited about a quarter of an hour when two of the boats astern came rushing up out of the darkness. We all went ahead again. I could just make out five in sight. During this part of our journey we had been hugging the Finnish shore, and could see quite plainly the beach and forest behind it.

11.45 p.m. Altered course for Kronstadt and soon lost sight of the land on our port side. Boats astern were dropping behind and only three could be now seen. After about half an hour's run, land could be seen to starboard which we knew was Kronstadt (Konin) Island. We ran on for some miles and then the first fortress loomed up. Strange to say, this fort was not marked on our chart. We were getting quite close to the Island and now sighted the chain of small forts which guard the Petrograd Bay. They rise right out of the sea and look unpleasantly close together. We seemed to be in sight of these forts for an interminably long time; I began to feel quite drowsy and had to keep awake by constantly reminding myself that any instant those black objects might change into flashes of gunfire. Indeed the noise our engines were making, and later from the large sheets of flames coming out of the exhaust-pipes of the boat ahead (Dobson and MacBean) we ought to have been spotted at any minute.

Only two other boats could be seen, but we knew it was too late to slow down for the remainder. Our reduced number made one feel slightly less safe, as the programme had been made on the assumption that all boats would arrive. Kronstadt Island was only a few miles off on our starboard beam. The first large fort was now behind and the chain of forts through which we had now to pass were only a few hundred yards away.

12.50 a.m. Passed between forts 7 and 10. The seconds seemed like hours; it appeared outside all possibility that they would not see us. I stood by the Lewis gun, pointing at the fort as we passed – not that it would be of much use, but it gave one confidence.

1 a.m. At last we were inside the forts and at the back of Kronstadt Island. The lights of Petrograd could be seen distinctly in the distance. Boats now formed in line ahead in the order of Bremner No.1, MacBean No.2, with Dobson on board, Dayrell-Reed No.3. We steered for the middle of the entrance to the dockyard basin.

The air raid was now in progress and searchlights were being switched on from various positions, bursts of shrapnel could be seen as well as tracer ammunition from the planes as they dived on the searchlights, also an occasional red flame when a bomb had been dropped. We knew by this that our faithful supporters – the Air Force – were taking the enemy's attention off us and getting a warm reception themselves in consequence.

1.10 a.m. We rounded the point at the end of the island; there was a small fort on it. Everything seemed quite peaceful and nobody awake. The aerial bombardment had now ceased and we slowed down to make less noise. The entrance to middle harbour could now be seen to starboard and ahead of us the guard-ship. She looked quite peaceful at anchor and it was hard to imagine her as an enemy ship guarding the entrance to any enemy harbour.

One CMB (Napier) and an aeroplane had been detailed to attack her, but they had not arrived she was left to herself and one after another our three CMB's glided past her in single line ahead. I have a recollection that McBean gave her a burst of machine-gun fire as he passed but am not certain. Nothing seemed to happen, however, and we arrived at the dock entrance without a shot being fired at us. We stopped engines to give the two boats ahead of us (Bremner and McBean) time to get in. Suddenly a huge bump and dull thud was felt – I knew a ship had been torpedoed. The next instant a high column of water could be seen rising from the side of a cruiser (battle ship) with three funnels and two masts. She was quite close to us.

Bremner (No.1) had found his target, and the *Pamiat Azova* listed rapidly on her side. After this there was a silence and still no sign of life. The air bombardment had obviously driven everybody underground. We entered the harbour. Then fire was opened upon us, first from the direction of the dry dock, and afterwards from other sides. We followed behind Dobson, heading for the corner where our objectives the battleships were berthed. Almost simultaneously we received bursts of fire in the boat from the batteries and splashes now appeared on both sides. Morley and I instinctively ducked for a moment as the bullets whistled past; when I looked up, I could see splashes everywhere in the basin. I turned round and was just about to remark to Dayell-Reed 'Where are you heading?' (as we were making straight for the hospital ship), when I noticed that, although still standing up and holding the wheel, his head was resting on the wooden conning tower top in front of him. I lowered him into the cockpit, at the same time I put the wheel hard over and righted the boat on her proper course. We were quite close to the battleship *Andrei Pervozvanni*. I must fire now or never. In a few seconds it would be too late. Throttling back the engines as far as possible I fired both torpedoes at her after which I stopped one engine to help turn the boat quickly.

Almost as I did this we saw two columns of water rise up from the side of the battleship and heard two crashes. I knew they must have been Dobson's torpedoes which had found their target. We now headed for our billet which was close to the hospital ship but, while turning, there was a terrific explosion nearby. We received a great shock and a douche of water. Looking over my shoulder I realised the cause of it was one of our torpedoes exploding on the side of the battleship. We were so close to her that a shower of picric powder from the warhead of our torpedo was thrown over the stern of the boat, staining us a yellow colour which we had some difficulty in removing afterwards when we reached Biorko.

Continuing on we missed a lighter near the hospital ship luckily by a few feet only and afterwards followed Dobson out of the basin entrance. I had just time to take another look back over my shoulder to see the result of our second torpedo. A high column of flame from the battleship lit up the whole basin. We passed the guard-ship at anchor – Morley gave her a burst of machine-gun fire as a partying present, and afterwards went to see what he could do for Reed. We bandaged his head and gave him a morphia pill.

We could see Bremner's boat being blown up at this stage. Her petrol tank must have caught fire as there were large flames all around her. The forts through which we had to pass on our return now commenced firing at us with light Q.F. stuff as well as machine guns. We rattled on to full speed and were getting it badly when McBean ahead made a smoke screen in which we got relief. Their searchlights now began to play upon us. Closer and closer the beams came until they fund us, when luckily, instead of holding us in their beams they seemed to switch off to something else, or else in the air. I think probably on to our aircraft.

Reed nearly recovered consciousness at one time and tried to speak. We shook hands with him in turn and I think he knew the boat had done well. Soon we were near Biorko and saw a destroyer and asked for a doctor but they had none. Luckily the flagship was close by, and when we got alongside her the Admiral came down from the bridge to speak to us, and also Reed, who died soon afterwards. Eventually we got alongside the old *Vindictive*. They gave us a cheer.

Gordon Steele reported in the *Daily Telegraph* on 7 April 1920:

If ever a Victoria Cross was well earned, it was this one given for sinking a Bolshevik cruiser (battleship). One can only wonder how even one or two men from civilised countries can be so deluded as to have any truck with that blood-thirsty a debase ruffian Lenin, who holds rule by violence in a so-called "free" country, where labour is conscripted, where it literally is a crime punishable with death to have moderately clean hands, where men and women alike have sunk far below the level of the beasts of the field, and where not only aristocracy but middle and working classes are at the peril of their lives, ground under the heel of criminal lunatic or worse.

Gus Agar condensed his narrative in his book, *Baltic Episode* written in 1963, some forty years after the raid. He had been cautioned not to write about his part in the attack.

It was quite dark and nearly 10.30 pm by the time Dobson made his flashlight signal to 'Go on'. I could see Napier quite clearly behind me, and another boat behind him whose exhaust pipes were giving out terrific flashes as one engine back-fired at intervals. Not a happy start I thought but soon she quietened down. We were doing about an easy twenty knots as we approached the forts, and had lost sight of those astern except Napier. We thought we could see three of them half a mile away on our starboard side throwing up spray from their bow waves. Napier behind us was also throwing up a lot of spray and I was certain there was little chance of our making the passages through the forts unobserved, as the boat behind him had a badly tuned engine making a fearful din and spitting out flames from her exhaust. It was just too bad, but nothing could be done about it except crack on speed when the forts opened fire, which they did. Luckily their searchlights were not switched on and the fire, which was light battery and machine gun stuff, was extremely haphazard and did no damage except top our smuggler-pilot's morale.

We went on a wide circle towards Petrograd main channel before turning towards Kronstadt dockyard, having lost sight of those on our starboard side whom were assumed had gone through the other passage of the inner forts.

It transpired afterwards that Dobson and the two boats following him (Bremner and Dayrell-Reed) lost sight of us in the darkness. His smuggler-pilot finding himself too close to the northern end of the Kronstadt shore, turned parallel to the chain of forts slipping in close to either Nos. 7 or 10. A gap we had not previously used, on which they would certainly have stuck, had it not been for the extra three feet of water under their propellers.

Actually because of their spray they were sighted by the large fortress of Kotlin guarding the northern shore, and were given several bursts of fire but again, as with our party, there was no damage because Kotlin failed to switch on their searchlights and all CMBs, except No.6 (Howard) successfully got through the passages. Howard had to be left behind and was picked up later by Bodley (No.7) on his way back from the basin when both came under heavy fire: a splendid combination of bravery and seamanship and a lucky escape for the *Rurik* which was Howard's target.

So far luck was on our side. First, because of the Pilot's mistake, Dobson with his first three attacking boats was able to cut the corner and get a shorter passage to the basin. Thus placed him well ahead of the second party to follow and he arrived at the entrance of the basin with time to spare. Secondly, the extra water level had certainly helped his boats to get through a passage we had never tried before, and lastly the Russians never used their searchlights which could have been our undoing, perhaps because they were not ready-manned or because they did not want to give away their position to our airmen. It is impossible to say. They were certainly in good working order, as was proved the following day and afterwards. Luck, however, is two sided and it later broke back on us.

On arrival off the basin entrance complete surprise was thus achieved and Walter Cowan's plan succeeded beyond expectations, the rest was up to the CMBs. There was no boom in place or obstruction to be blown up and no outward opposition whatsoever. Our RAF friends, the airboys, were doing their stuff most gallantly upstairs, zooming around and dropping their small bombs as near as possible to the batteries on the breakwaters whose gunners were obviously taking cover. We could see the red flashes of the bombs as they exploded. Bill Bremner (No.1) had a clear run in and a straight target for the *Pamiat Azova* which he got with his one and only torpedo – a bull's-eye – followed as he described, by a crunching roar as the sound of the explosion reverberated across the water to where we were waiting, a quarter of a mile off the Military Harbour to stop any patrol craft that might come out.

Bremner then went over to his waiting billet and was soon followed by Dobson (No.2). His was a very difficult manoeuvre because, to get in position to fire his torpedoes, he had to stop one engine, turn the boat, and gather speed rapidly before firing, a task which required much skill and judgement, but 'Beans' at the wheel was an experienced hand and had the boat steadied and on course exactly at the right moment when Dobson fired, scoring two bull's-eyes on the *Andrei Pervozvanni* followed by two terrific explosions and proceeded to his waiting billet near the hospital ship to wait for Dayrell-Reed (No.3). By this time the basin had thoroughly woken up and was alive with general pandemonium and confusion. Searchlights were sweeping the water indiscriminately and Russian machine-guns making their horrible typewrite sounds were click-clacking all over the place regardless of where they were firing provided it was a moving target. Into this came 'Mossy' Reed (No.3) and Brade (No.4). Our boats replied with their Lewis guns which were fitted with belts of RASF tracer ammunition, though this turned out to be a liability as tracer bullets gave away their position.

'Mossy' had been in CMBs ever since their start in late 1917 and had been well trained in boat handling by Eric Wellman. Nothing ever moved him and I can see him now with his head sticking over the canvas screen shielding the torpedo firing instrument and steering wheel. Following the same technique as Dobson and Russell McBean his boat had to make an even sharper turn towards his target before gathering speed to fire, but with expert skill and superb judgement he had the turn started perfectly, when something happened, and instead of righting the wheel to allow for the swing, the boat continued on turning with 'Mossy' slumped over the wheel making no effort at all to check it.

Real moments of crisis are rare and this was one of them. To act swiftly and correctly on split second judgement with a cool head, when bullets and shells are flying around and any moment may be the last on this earth, requires both physical courage and temperament which few possess. In Gordon Steele, his second in command, 'Mossy' had such a one. Turning around from the shoulder of his Lewis gun, Gordon realised at once that the boat was off course and out of control. 'Mossy' had been shot in the head. Jumping to the wheel and levers, he brought the boat under control again and carried out the attack against the *Petropavlovsk* as originally planned, firing his torpedoes so close that one hit the heavy cable by which the battleship was made fast, part of the yellow picric powder from the explosion of the torpedo falling on the stern of the CMB. The other torpedo struck the forward part of the huge ship underneath the turret, putting her out of action.

Agar and the rest of the crews of the CMBs, buried 'Mossy' Reed the next day in the tiny Finnish cemetery at Koivisto with full naval honours from the fleet. It was all the more moving when two little girls ran out from the crowd of village spectactors with posies of wild fowers for his grave. We learned later that that the Russians had also buried the bodies of our naval seamen due largely to the Bolshevik Commissar Gordienko, who had been a petty officer on the tsar's Royal Yacht, *Standart.*

Gordon then joined Dobson at the waiting billet following him out of the basin entrance. And through the chain of forts which by this time were already for the boats on their return journey with searchlights as well as their QF staff. But by making a smoke screen ahead, and with the aid of our airmen who came to their support diving fearlessly onto the forts with their tracer bullets going full blast, the CMBs managed to get through without serious damage. Both Dobson's and Steele's boats (Nos.2 and 3) were intercepted by the flagship on their way to Biorko and the wounded 'Mossy' transferred to the cruiser's sick-bay. He died soon afterwards but not before the Admiral spoke to him and shook his hand, as did all members of his crew.

Dobson in *CMB-31BD* had drawn alongside the hospital ship which was tied to the harbour wall and waited for Steele's CMB to draw alongside. When it was clear, they headed back to Biorko. Gus Agar in *CMB-7* was waiting outside the entrance to the Main harbour. As the only 40-footer, he had one torpedo to fire. He remained waiting until the surviving boats had fired their torpedoes. He stayed for a considerable time but failed to find out what happened to *CMB-62BD*, *CMB-24A* and *CMB-79A*. As he was the last to leave, he decided to fire his torpedo into the small Military harbour in the hopes that he would hit some small transport. He came under heavy fire until a lone aeroplane chose to divert the searchlight beams away from Agar. Flight Lieutenant Albert 'Fletch' Fletcher, RNAS flew his Short seaplane and dived his aeroplane down the beam of the searchlights, strafing the emplacements with bullets, enabling Agar to escape. For this act he was awarded the OBE. The smallest of the three harbours contained patrol boats and tugs which were bunched together opposite the narrow entrance. With the other CMBs occupied with the warships, Agar decided to fire his only torpedo into the Military harbour in the hopes of hitting something. Accelerating, he turned his craft to port, made a 360-degree circuit and sped for the opening. He fired his torpedo, immediately turned to starboard and made in the direction of the Petrograd Channel. He heard his explosion, which must have caused some damage. Gus Agar concentrated of firing into what he hoped was a mass of patrol boats moored to the quay. The torpedo had been aimed at the densest concentration of patrol vessels although he could not see what he was firing at. While he did not see the torpedo strike, he did hear the explosion followed by several secondary explosions. It was noted that no Bolshevik patrol boats emerged from the Military harbour during the raid.

*CMB-24* commanded by Sub-Lieutenant Lawrence Napier was given the task of sinking the guard ship, *Gavril*. For some reason he missed; either the torpedo went under the ship or it hit an object in the water, diverting it. *CMB-24* was hit by a large-calibre shell from the *Gavril* or one of the batteries on the harbour wall, splitting the boat in half. Sub-Lieutenant Osman Horton Giddy described what happened.

As Agar's boat, which was leading us, turned in its tracks opposite the basin entrance – this was the prearranged signal that we were in position – a score or so of batteries opened fire from what appeared to be every possible direction. We swung hard over to the right and headed straight for the outline of the guard-ship. We must have been quite close because Napier fired his torpedo as soon as we came out of the turn. We had no chance to watch for its success; there was a sudden rush of flame and a noise which split the surrounding pandemonium into nothing. I felt a sharp jab in my back and I fell across the cockpit.

There followed the most amazing silence broken ridiculously by the voice of our Welsh mechanic, 'That's sugared it.' Although I did not know it, Napier had been blown into the water. I was about to jump below to get the engines restarted when I saw that our boat had been split in half longitudinally. With my two seaman I tried to free two Kapok fenders to form a raft and was about to do so when *CMB24A* (official number of our boat) subsided gently under our feet and we stepped off the disappearing hull into the waters of the Gulf of Finland …

So much had happened in the last five minutes that I felt little interest in my own situation, but with eagerness I watched the harbour mouth into which our CMB's had disappeared. Soon a huge flame rose above the searchlights which was followed by heavy explosions and implied that things were getting really busy. I could see the destroyer guard-ship more plainly anchored off the entrance, and I realised that our torpedo had missed. She must have seen our bobbing heads in the water for soon the machine-gun sprayed bullets around us. We made comic attempts to dive underwater but I soon discovered that my body was dead below the waist. No one was hit and the destroyers attention diverted by the exit of two of our boats from the basin at full speed with tracer bullets from their machine-guns turned on the destroyer like meteors fired from the sky … I was a good sight from the water and I became semi-conscious in the water, but was supported by my life jacket to be awaked about two hours later by the form of a grey row boat with white figures in her. For all I cared thy might have been the boatmen of the Styx.

In the midst of the chaos created by the first group, the second wave began its attempt. At the entrance to the main basin, Brade's incoming boat rammed Bremner's broadside on as it was exiting. Brade had been blinded by the searchlights, and instead of running straight on, had turned hard-left directly into *CMB-79*, which was coming from the waiting area on the left-hand end of the basin. Bremner, whose boat had come under heavy machine-gun fire while waiting to leave and who had been wounded seven times, boarded Brade's boat and took charge. He pushed the remains of *CMB-79* clear of the entrance and into the harbour. Returning to his own boat, Bremner rigged the gun cotton charges to blow up the boat. With his crew, he abandoned their wrecked CMB and joined the *CMB-62*. Seeing the guard ship still in action, Brade closed in on her and fired both torpedoes. They both missed, giving *Gavril* the chance to claim a second victim. She opened fire, and *CMB-62* was hit several times amidst a hail of gunfire and came to full stop with her engines failing. Only 200 yards from *Gavril,* the flimsy boat was blasted out of the water and the entire crew perished. The demolition charges went off and Bremner's and Brade's went up in a sheet of flame.

The only remaining attacker was Bodley's *CMB-72*, which was put out of action when the torpedo-firing gear had been shot away. Unable to join the attack, Bodley turned about and headed for safety. This proved to be a lucky break for Bodley as he spotted Howard in his broken-down *CMB-86* outside the North Channel sea wall. He came alongside and attached a line to the stricken boat while the searchlights played and the machine guns opened fire. Miraculously, both boats were hit but not sunk and Bodley managed to tow Howard's CMB back to Biorko.

As Agar sought to return to Terrioki, he was conscious of the fortresses being awake to the CMBs being trapped in the beam of a searchlight. It was fortunate that Flight-Lieutenant Albert Fletcher, RNAS, in a Short seaplane dived down the beam of the searchlight and strafed the fortress, keeping the enemy's heads down and distracting the searchlight until Agar could escape. Of the other airmen and their mish-mash of aircraft, Captain Randall was forced to make a landing in the sandy beach at Biorko due to engine failure but there were no fatalities among the air crews.

As soon as Donald's pilots acting as decoys had landed at Koivisto and refuelled their planes, they took off at sunrise to reconnoitre the harbour. They saw that the floating dock had been damaged by bombs from the earlier raid and they were jubilant on seeing the two battleships,

*Petropavlovsk* and *Andrei Pervozvanni* and the depot ship *Pamiat Azova* sunk, though there was insufficient water to submerge the hulls. Aerial photographs of Kronstadt harbour the next day revealed that the battleships lay on their sides, obviously out of action. The submarine depot ship had heeled over but most of her superstructure remained above water. In many ways the British naval force had achieved their gaol in a few minutes but the destruction of *CMB-62BD*, *CMB-24A* and *CMB-79A* had reduced the destruction of the Russian ships somewhat. A few days later *The Times* wrote an inaccurate report.

> Some details are now available of the dashing exploit of British coastal motor-boats in attacking the Bolshevik fleet and sinking two Bolshevik battleships and a destroyer (?). The motor-boats attacked without support of the fleet but accompanied by three (?) aeroplanes … The British losses were three boats sunk by gun-fire and one blown up by a mine … It is impossible to overestimate the debt of the Baltic States to the small and indefatigable squadron under Rear-Admiral Cowan. Had it not been there the Bolshevik warcraft would have ravaged Scandinavian water unchecked. It is not surprising that the Finns, recognising this, fail to comprehend why the Allies give no encouragement to Finland to take the sole step necessary to complete the security of northern Europe by the occupation of Petrograd.

Following the exploits at Kronstadt, Gordon Steele returned to more peaceful pursuits with the Royal Navy. In 1923 he took command of patrol boat No. 31 at Portland, and with his aptitude for languages, he became a naval interpreter in Russia. Due to his knowledge of submarines, he was appointed to Rear-Admiral of Submarine at Gosport. His last appointment was as first lieutenant of the new Royal Navy cruiser, HMS *Cornwall*, on which he served at the China Station from 1927 to 1928. This was the ship that went down with *Dorsetshire* in the Bay of Bengal in 1942. He was then selected to the post of captain superintendent of HMS *Worcester*, a position he held from 1929 to his retirement in 1957. He fully expected wartime duties with the Royal Navy but he was not called upon to take a position on a wartime ship.

On 20 January 1958 Steele was the subject of the BBC programme *This is Your Life*, hosted by Eamon Andrews. During the programme he was introduced to Captain E. R. Bodley, who commanded *CMB-72* as a sub-lieutenant during the attack of Kronstadt harbour. Bodley had joined the P&O Company and retired as commodore in 1957. Gordon Steele died in his ninetieth year on 4 January 1981, and was buried at Winkleigh, Devon.

Around late summer, *CMB-4* made its last trip. A Bolshevik agent threw a hand grenade into the garden of Villa Sakharov, which blew in a few broken panes and caused a large hole in the garden. The commandant was indignant and immediately posted a guard outside the *dacha*. Admiral Cowan received a message from Cumming instructing the crew to cease all Secret Service activity and to use Terrioki as a liaison base. In September 1919 Agar remained and teamed up with Russell McBean in the 55ft *CMB-31* and went south of Kronstadt. Here they made for the main channel, which the Bolsheviks had made mine-free. With the small bombs that were laid in the troughs of the CMB, the two men laid a cluster of bombs in the main channel. This was mainly to prevent the Russian warships using the main channel in their attack on the Estonian port of Revel. After the *Gavril*, which stood as the guard ship outside Kronstadt harbour, emerged from the harbour with another destroyer, the *Azard*, to patrol the Finnish Gulf, the *Azard*, commanded by Tzarist officers, was sunk off Luga Bay. Seven crew managed to escape to the Estonian side. Unfortunately, the ships were commanded by White Russian naval officers and both met their end in the channel, having decided to surrender to the Royal Navy. Some crew managed to escape from the mines and reach the shore. They then crossed the frontier to the combined forces of the Whites and Estonians.

The original mission was now finished. Agar telephoned Sindall and told him to remain in Terrioki, gather any information and check up on the position of the prisoners captured during the Kronstadt Raid. The Soviet wireless station omitted any mention of the sinking of their fleet but did crow about sinking three CMBs and capturing four officers and six ratings. Agar was ordered home on 16 September 1919 to receive his Victoria Cross. He travelled to Helsingfors, where he was given the Legation Despatches and a diplomatic passport. As an official messenger, he travelled to Stockholm and received another foreign bag, which he took to the Foreign Office.

He had a lengthy interview with the Lords of the Admiralty before taking a train to his friends at Blairgowrie, near Balmoral. Unfortunately, his Scottish visit to receive his Victoria Cross was aborted. Owing to a railway strike, there were no trains to return to London, except for an emergency service, which he managed to catch and arrive back in London. He was invited at 10.30 am on 9 October 1919 to be presented with his Victoria Cross and the additional Distinguished Service Order in a private meeting at Buckingham Palace.

In April an exchange was arranged and the naval personnel were able to leave Russia. As Cowan's flagship, *Caledon*, departed for England, the cruiser *Curacoa* arrived and on 7 May he transferred his flag to her. Having met Mannerheim in Helsingfors, Cowan left for a quick visit to Libau. On the morning of 13 May, 70 miles east of Revel, they struck a mine. Cowan was in his cold bath at the time and donning an overcoat, hurried to the bridge. He found that the damage had occurred to the right aft where several compartments had been flooded. He also lost a rating killed and several officers injured. Limping into Revel, he again transferred his flag to *Cleopatra* while temporary repairs were made to *Curocoa*. On 24 May the *Galatea* arrived at Revel carrying General Hubert Gough. On 5 June Cowan was granted permission by the Finnish government to anchor his fleet on Biorko Sound.

# Chapter Fourteen

# Agar's Return to the Baltic

When Admiral Cowan was told of the capture of the prisoners left behind at Kronstadt, he was most concerned. Agar informed the Foreign Office, who contacted the Danish Red Cross and hoped there would be an exchange. The raid had stirred up a hornet's nest and the Bolsheviks redoubled their efforts to stamp out all opposition. Inside Petrograd, thousands of people were arrested and many were executed for no other reason than for not being actively supportive of the Bolsheviks. Gangs of the Cheka were out in the streets, arresting the innocent and invading the houses of the people who had nothing to do with politics. The Bolsheviks were well aware of the small naval presence at Terrioki, for they sent two aircraft to drop bombs on the village, which made the naval party unpopular with the locals. Despite this flurry of activity, Augustus Agar knew that he had to try one more time to bring out 'ST25'.

The Kronstadt forts were now on full alert and Agar knew it was hopeless to try and creep through the incomplete breakwaters at low speed. Instead, he decided that he would speed through Forts 7 and 8. Although he saw searchlights sweeping the approaches to the other forts, there were no searchlights from No. 8. A month after the Kronstadt Raid, Agar took the 55ft CMB and laid a cluster of mines in the main shipping channel to Petrograd. Ironically, the *Gavril* would become a victim of one of the mines, sinking in the shallows and blocking the channel. The fate of Kronstadt and the militant sailors of the Baltic Fleet were equally tragic. Having defended the Revolution, the sailors became disenchanted with what they felt was a new dictatorship centralized in Moscow's Communist Party. In March 1921 they were determined to preserve the local power of the Kronstadt Revolutionary Committee. Ignoring ultimatums from Lenin, Kronstadt was attacked by the Red Army troops. Leon Trotsky demanded a series of reforms, which included a reduction in the Bolshevik power, newly-elected Soviet councils, economic freedom for peasants and workers, dissolution of the bureaucratic government voice during the revolution and restoration of the working class. This was something Lenin and his supporters refused to comply with. When Joseph Stalin took control and began his Great Purge during the 1930s, Trotsky left Russia. Hundreds of soldiers perished on the frozen ice of the Gulf of Finland in a futile attempt to storm the fort's batteries. After a two-week siege more than 50,000 Red Army fighters attacked Kronstadt's 15,000 defenders. In two days of heavy fighting – much of it from house to house in the old town – Kronstadt fell. More than 10,000 Red Army soldiers and 2,000 sailors died. Another 2,500 Kronstadters were captured and sent to camps in Siberia. Some 8,000 managed to escape across the ice to internment in Finland.

Agar found his two couriers of great use, and he was able to employ Peter Sokolov and a new man, Midshipman A. Gefter, to carry secret messages via Helsingfors to London. Paul Dukes adopted a new identity and disguised himself as a draughtsman named Alexander Bankau. He enlisted in the Red Army, and through one of his military agents was put in touch with the senior officer in the 8th Army. He was seconded to the Automobile Section, which – surprisingly – did not have any cars or lorries. Instead, he was given free rein to find petrol, tyres and motor spares for the non-existing vehicle section! The only English woman he had been in touch with was Laura Cade and she was on the point of being picked up by the Cheka in Petrograd. Dukes told Peter that he needed to get her out. One evening in February 1920, Peter appeared at her flat and told her to pack her suitcase and prepare to be smuggled out of Petrograd. They travelled to one of the islands to the north of Petrograd and caught a smuggler's sleigh to take her across the Gulf of Petrograd to Finland. During the journey, she got frostbite and had to recouperate in Finland.

Around 10 August Dukes learned that a new courier was hiding in Petrograd. He made contact with Gefter and the contrast with Peter was striking. Older than Peter, he was an ex-midshipman, a prize fighter, an artist and an actor. Dukes described him as a cocky, thick-set little man; very brave and self-assured. The writing of the naval cadet and courier, A. Gefter, was published in Germany in 1920 under the title *Reminiscences of a Courier – Archives of the Russian Revolution*. His grammar was somewhat mysterious but he did manage to explain himself. He set out to recall the adventures he had as courier in the two CMBs at Terrioki.

Two days later I was again in Terrioki. I had to go to Petrograd again to fetch the mysterious Englishman in the speedboat. This time, with the tall, fair sailor in command – Agar by name. Now the circumstances had changed and the condition of the passage was much harder. The matter was that owing to the English attack on Kronstadt with motor boats, the Bolsheviks had put up a number of powerful searchlights on the shore at Lissy Nos, on the batteries near Kronstadt, on Fort Obruchev, at Oranmenbaum and at Kasnaya Gorka. The whole gulf was in their lighted control.

They were also much disturbed by the innumerable attacks of the English airmen and were unable to sleep calmly at night. All this tended to disturb Agar's calm confidence which he had before, in making the passage between the forts. However, a start had none the less to be made, and the mysterious Englishmen would be waiting at midnight near Kamenny Island.

'Do you know, Gefter,' he said, 'I don't at all like the look of those searchlights'. We were walking through the woods, as before, to the little harbour at Terrioki from where we were to embark in his speedboat. 'If three of them catch us at the same time, there will be no escape. It will be devilishly easy for them to shoot at us.' I, however, was of a different opinion. Who could do us any harm in our wonderful speedboat which flew through the water like a magic carpet? It would have been quite another matter in an old tarred fishing boat, leaking with water.

When we put to sea, the narrow and seemingly feeble beam of a searchlight could be seen coming from Lissy Nos. Another beam from one of the Kronstadt batteries, but that was not a harmless beam. We reached a position which judged to be abreast of Sestoretsk, when suddenly the motionless beam of light jumped and swayed about over the water. It did not reach the sky, it searched only the water. Several times it slipped over the speedboat without observing it. Agar gave full speed. The motor groaned and cut the tips of the waves in anger. Suddenly a huge wall of water coloured with all the colours of the rainbow, and dazzling in its brightness blew up on the port side. The eyes could not stand for it. Three more searchlights discovered us. Ahead, out of a fort, a horizontal lightning flash flew out, and we heard a low thunder shaking the air.

We were being fired upon. At full speed, Agar turned to the right. For a few moments we were out of the beams. They ran to and fro over the water like the feelers of (H.G.) Well's Martians, but found the boat again. Agar changed the course once more. It was now out of the question to try to get through the forts. We must turn round them and back to Terrioki. For a considerable time succeeded in keeping himself out of the line of the lights and cheating them by changing his course. The searchlights, however, were still on the boat and were also scanning our earlier tracks. Not far from Fort Obruchev we were discovered by another searchlight from Kronstadt. It was so close that it literally blinded us with light. Agar turned aside, the beam followed, Agar changed the course again, but could no longer escape the light. The beam hung on to us like a Borzoi on to a wolf.

It was too near and we lost the course during the beating about … There was a dreadful blow and the sound of tearing iron accompanied also by the sound of broken glass. The motor stopped, and the beam of the searchlight, travelling with the boat's speed, rushed ahead. It lost us, this time for good, but the boat was sitting on something. There was a dead silence. I expected every moment that water would burst in and we should all go the bottom. But that did not happen. Where were we? I looked around. There were lights on the right, to the left and behind us. I went to the stern. The boat was held by the very end of the stern on a high cement breakwater which it was trying to take like a racehorse takes a jump.

The sudden halt of the boat knocked out Agar and Beeley. Agar came to on the floor of the cockpit. He could see Beeley slumped over the engine but he, too, began to regain consciousness. The whole crew were aware that that they had hit a breakwater close to Kotlin Island and that they had to get off the obstruction.

We pushed the boat with boathooks and after sometime she slid into the water and floated. We tried to start the motor but the starter would not work and when the engine was examined by an electric torch wrapped round in a handkerchief, it was found that there was no hope, for it was broken into two parts by the force of the collision. It was nearly midnight, and in less than four hours it would be dawn, when we would be taken off by the Bolsheviks.

Only a little bit of life remained to us and I knew that I should then have to share the lot of the sailors at Kronstadt who had been drowned with weights tied to their feet. My companions expected nothing better either. After a short consultation the following resolution was carried: if the Bolsheviks should come to take us in the morning, we should blow up the boat which contained a charge of dynamite for this very purpose.

I was given a lifebelt with which I might swim to the shore, but I refused it. At such moment I was strangely calm and clear-headed. We had four hours, so I suggested that we should rest for an hour or two to get up strength which we might still need to save ourselves later. I lay down in the boat and slept sweetly and awake with the rocking of the boat. I rubbed my eyes. Had a miracle happened? Definitely the lights were in a different place, they were farther away. Yes, we were drifting and in the right direction towards to the Finnish coast.

A fresh breeze began to blow from the south, blowing us to safety. It was necessary to make a sail, but first to turn the boat stern to the wind. We had not only no oars, but even no boards or planks with which we could have turned ourselves round. A floating anchor! We emptied some petrol tins and closed them hermetically. On the long end of a rope the cans were let out from the stern and, gradually pulling up and letting out the end, I succeeded in making the boat turn round into a line of waves. Then a long mast was hoisted from the deck. Two pieces of cloth were fastened to it and also to the motor. The sail was not a stylish one, but the boat sailed gaily along.

At sunrise we found ourselves quite a distance from the fortresses, it was a sunny day and the wind was freshening. The waves shook apart the damaged keel and the boat was leaking badly. Our nerves began to fail us, and the crew, who had not ceased to be on watch all night, working to get the water out of the boat, now began to show signs of weariness.

The fort hung over the water behind us. It seemed to hang on account of the morning refraction which causes a mirage. This gladdens me, for so must also, I thought, our boat appeared from the fort, as a strange object. Besides the boat painted with protective colours, and I had confidence that we should escape observation. I regained my nerves, but what was bad was that water was coming in, in spite of the fact that the crew had kept on pumping and working without a stop. It was unbelievable that, after escaping in the night, we should perish during the day, in perfect weather and in sight of the Finnish shore.

Despite of their frantic bailing, the boat continued to sink further in the water. Their progress was painfully slow and – with the eastern current – they only made about 2 knots. Still within sight of the forts they were suddenly enveloped in a mist which hid them. They also heard the sound of a small motor and suddenly a small fishing boat appeared. Suspicious of the boat, the fishermen began to pull away. Agar nodded to Marshall, who sent a burst of Lewis gunfire across the fishermen's boat and this certainly brought them back beside the sinking CMB. Fortuitously, they were landed at Terrioki.

The sky was cloudless and I saw an aeroplane appear in the sky. Agar lay exhausted at the wheel and the crew were also exhausted, would not have to fight an aeroplane. Mechanically, with expressionless faces they set to work to get ready the machine guns, but another miracle happened for an aeroplane could be seen quite clearly with the rings of the Allies painted on it. We regained fresh hope and new strength. More petrol cans were prepared for baling by knocking out the bottom of the cans and two small fishing boats suddenly appeared. They came a certain distance from us and stopped, but after threatening them with fire from the machine guns, one of them came alongside. They said that they had thought our boat was a British aeroplane which had crashed into the water.

A mast and sail were taken from one of the boats which we hoisted in our own instead of the ragged affair we had been using and the fishing boat was now directed to tow us towards the Finnish shore. Two hours later we were all safely home.

Agar carried another courier/agent, who had no sooner appeared than he vanished. His name was Kroslov, an officer who looked like an intellectual, wearing a *pince-nez* and a suit. Around the second week of August, Dukes learned that Gefter was to be found in a safe house. Gefter told Dukes that he had left his skiff in the reeds on the outskirts of Lakhta, a suburb of Petrograd. On 14 August Dukes collected his reports from both Aunt Natalia and Klachonka. A rather mysterious female had entered Dukes' circle named Petrovskaya, who may have been either Aunt Natalia or Klachonka. She had collected the money from George Gibson to keep the network running but then seemed to have vanished. By this time, Gus Agar and his crew had finished their mission at Terrioki. The *CMB-7* was a sunken wreck and was towed outside the harbour to be destroyed by guncotton. *CMB-4* still had life left in her and was taken to Biorko Sound for repairs. While at Terrioki harbour, two Bolshevik aeroplanes flew over but dropped their bombs in the surrounding forest. The Russian émigrés said the pilots had White sympathies and had deliberately jettisoned them in the woods away from the harbour. The commandant was distressed at the incident and posted a guard to keep a watch on the crew's house. Agar assigned Sindall to become 'ST35' to act as liaison officer, while Marshall and Beeley travelled to Biorko Sound in case *CMB-4* was ready for further service. News came that Dukes, Peter and Kostya had made it into Latvia, which gave Agar time to carry out one more mission, this time for Admiral Cowan.

Agar left Helsingfors on 16 September, wearing his brown suit which he had bought from Moss Bros. He was performing the role of a King's Messenger and was given Legation Despatches and a diplomatic passport. The next day Agar sailed to Stockholm. He spotted General Mannerheim at the stern and noticed that Mannerheim watched his native land gradually disappear until it was dark. He then removed his hat, bowed and disappeared to his quarters. When Agar arrived at the dockside, he was greeted by Major John Scale 'ST24' and his wife and they had lunch together. Scale was all-affability but later complained to Mansfield Cumming that Gus Agar was 'very *difficile*' and that his agents, Le May and Hall, had got their way.

Having hours to catch a train, Agar spotted a poster advertising a football match between the Swedish Select XI and the United States champions, Bethlehem Steel, who were touring at that time. The match finished 3–2 to Bethlehem. His courier, Peter Petrovich, had been an excellent companion and was very reliable. He had played for the Russian team, and Agar thought he would dedicate the match in his honour. Afterwards, Agar was given a few despatches from Scale to take to London. Travelling by train to Bergen, he caught a steamer to Hull, where he was picked up by a chauffeur and taken to London.

# Chapter Fifteen

# Dukes' Departure from Petrograd

Paul Dukes had managed to disguise himself with about twenty different aliases. These included Joseph Afirenko, Joseph Krylenko, Alexander Markovich, Sergei Ilitch, Ivan Ivanich, John Johnovich, Alexander Bankau and Vladimir Piotrovsky (dead soldier). He had managed to avoid the Cheka but instead had joined the Communist Party. Dukes managed to do the rounds of his friends and say his goodbyes. Some he was unable to meet ever since the Orlov affair; the Doctor had gone to a private practice on Vasily Island, Sonia Marenko was still in Deryabinsky prison and a Russian officer was most contrite having turned Dukes from his apartment and later executed. The communists were told that Dukes had left a message saying he was visiting relatives without leaving an address. He spent his last day with Aunt Natalia and Klachonka, two of his best agents. One night in January 1920, Aunt Natalia was arrested with another group of prisoners and taken to a town east of Petrograd. She was machine-gunned together with the other prisoners and thrown into an unmarked pit. Klachonka was a nurse at the hospital and was very clever at covering up Dukes from the Cheka.

Gefter had arrived near to Staraya Derevnya in the *CMB-4* and rowed ashore, hiding the skiff in the reeds. He could not find it again; between Lakhta and Petrograd, the reeds at that part of the coast extended 2 or 3 miles and there were no distinguishing landmarks. Dukes met up with Gefter in Petrograd and they decided to leave the city together and board Agar's boat. Unable to find his skiff, they found a fisherman who agreed to an exchange of a large supply of potatoes from a speculator in exchange for the fishing boat as he had been restricted to fishing in the Bay by the Bolsheviks. He led the pair to find his fishing boat at Lissy Nos opposite Kronstadt. The idea was to row back east to a spot south of the Elgin lightship and evade the coastal patrol.

Dukes caught the train from the Finland Station and Gefter sat with him. They were dressed in army clothes and had plenty to eat, much to the envy of the other passengers. They got off at Razdielnaya, halfway to the Finnish frontier, and made their way eastwards to the fisherman's hut. As dusk was falling around 10.00 pm, they were taken to the fishing boat, which had been rowed to the reeds. It was a fair-sized boat with three rowing benches and a large locker forming the seat at the stern. The fisherman carried the two agents to the fishing boat and they began to row eastwards. They struggled with the rowing, and with a storm brewing, they could make no headway. Gefter went to the stern, opened the locker and exclaimed that the fish-well was full to the brim with water. With nothing to bail it out with, the two men tried to row but the locker became submerged. Turning towards the shore, they perched on the prow and saw the shoreline half a mile away. At that moment, Gefter removed his top boots, much to Dukes' dismay, and said he could not swim in them.

As the boat disappeared beneath the waves, the two men struck out for the reeds. Despite being encumbered by their army clothing, they managed to reach the shore, where they rested awhile. They were both lucky as there was a lack of patrols along the shore due to slackened vigilance. Deciding to reach the fisherman's hut, they clambered through the reeds and woods for an hour. Gefter's feet were bloodied and he could not go on without help. Then a gunshot rang out and guards passed by without spotting the two men. Gefter was completely done in and unconscious. Dukes could not do anything and began to rub Gefter's feet and apply artificial respiration until he began to revive. Knowing that the patrols did not search all night, Dukes half carried Gefter along the sandy paths and eventually arrived at the fisherman's hut, where he left him to recover.

Gefter appeared a couple of days later in the fisherman's boots and was guilty of 'criminal negligence' for not checking the fish-locker. Within a few moments, he reasserted his self-assurance. Dukes was rather glad he had not made the trip, and gave Gefter his despatches so he could travel through Estonia. Dukes now travelled to Moscow and as a full-blown member of the Communist Party, he travelled first class. He met up with the counter-revolutionary society named the National Centre, but sadly it was infiltrated and all 500 members were executed.

Shura Marenko made his appearance after four months of travel through Murmansk and Finland and joined one of the White Russian armies to take revenge for the death of Sonia, his wife. She succumbed to the ravages of hunger and famine, being held captive during the harsh winter of 1919. Another system was compelling the peasants by force to give up their grain to the government, so the peasants resorted to killing the Bolshesvik emissaries and burying the grain in the ground. The result was – although the Government supplies increased – that the masses of people were left hungrier than before. Strikes broke out around the country and the Bolshevik Government was forced to allow the citizens to forage for food in the countryside. The Bolsheviks conceded the first official free trading – the 'capitalist wedge' – into the communist system.

While in Moscow, he arranged a meeting with British chaplain Frank William North, one of the few representatives left, and by good fortune, passed on a list of British nationals, which he transmitted to the Foreign Office. The affairs of the British were conducted by the Swiss and Norwegian Missions, who let slip that they were working on behalf of the few British left in Moscow. North revealed that 'If we leave them alone and do not trade with them, I believe that the end of the Soviet rule is bound to come soon. Most of their transport is ruined, and the people are demoralised and refuse to work ... It is all one great mad-house.' The conditions in Moscow became one of robbery. The Bolsheviks had stolen his church funds, including a fund held for British people who were destitute. They stole his silver plate and chalices, and eventually took Mrs North's jewels as well. He stayed on at St. Andrews Church, but with a congregation of two or three, he finally left Moscow. Later, he sailed on the hospital ship *Dongola* and on 29 May 1920 he arrived at Waterloo Station with his wife and son, and other refugees. He was greeted by Paul Dukes on the platform and later received a well-merited award.

Preparing to leave Russia, Dukes was quietly told by his commanding officer, Vasili Petrovich, that the Red Army unit was being moved to Latvia. Dukes suggested that he would like to disappear when the time came and his commander suggested that he should be 'killed'. He had papers that had not gone through the process and he would be known as Vladimir Piotrovsky, a member of the Communist Party like Dukes. Joined by Peter, they were under orders to join an artillery brigade on the Latvian front. One sticking point was neither of them knew the part of the district they would travel. By ferreting around, Dukes found a young man whose family lived in the deep forest region.

The certificate obtained by Paul Dukes from the Bolshevist authorities when he served in the Red Army showed him to be a member of the automobile section of the 6th Army, under the name of Alexander Bankau, one of the many names he had assumed in Russia. The certificate says: 'The bearer of this, Bankau, Alexander, is in military service, Automobile Division. VIth Army, to which is appended his own signature, Bankau, and which is certified to by the following signatures and seals.' The certificate bears the letterhead: 'Russian Socialist Federated Soviet Republic, Automobile Division of the VIth Army.' It is dated May 25, 1919 in the town of Svatovo, and countersigned by the names of the chief of the Automobile Division, 6th Army, the political commissar in charge, and an official whose title may be translated as secretary-manager. The seals are those of the Automobile Division of the 6th Army. A photograph represents the disguise affected by Dukes when serving in the automobile section of the Red Army.

Finally taking his leave of his female agents, Aunt Natalia and Klachonka, he removed his intelligence from Natalia's family tomb and destroyed all but the most important documents. Dividing the intelligence into three, he chose to carry three bags of salt into which he hid the packets. In early September 1919, the three comrades, Paul Dukes, Peter Petrovich and the young man called Kostya, caught a train from Vitebsk Station which was packed tight. Peter managed to get through a window and wedged himself in, followed by the other two. For eleven hours, they spent the night squeezed among hordes of soldiers and foragers. They managed to doze until roused by the frequent stops the train made travelling about 200 miles south. Next day, they had to change trains and were confronted by a militiaman who demanded to know their business. The papers silenced him but he eyed the trio suspiciously, particularly the bags of salt. That evening they caught a train which was less crowded and secured half of a second-class coach, which they shared with another couple of soldiers. The train rumbled along, stopping at every station until it pulled into a siding. Kostya went to find out what was happening and came back with the news that the train was surrounded by militiamen. After speaking with the militiaman, they were convinced that they were about to be captured. Instead, they heard voices and footsteps in the other half of the second-class carriage but no one came near their coach.

They spent the next few dark hours in silence until an armed guard pulled the door open and asked where they were going and it would appear that all five soldiers were going to Rezhitsa. When they reached Rezhitsa, they joined the crush in the waiting room. Kostya went to look for a train to take them towards the Front. He gestured that they should catch the train which had a couple of box-cars with the doors open. They dashed across the tracks and managed to get on board before the train departed to Dvinsk. Kostya, who knew the area well, said they should travel 10 miles and then jump off as they reached an incline. As the train slowed, they were able to leap off and hide in a deep ditch. After the long journey, Kostya found a track which led them to a cottage where his cousins lived deep in the forest. Here they felt safe and were able to relax.

They awoke the next morning and Kostya's relatives had a horse and cart to take them to the shore of Lake Lubans, the frontier of the war between the Red Army and the Latvians. At last they came to a fringe of the forest and could see the lake a mile or so in the distance. A straight track ran through the bog on either side and the trio ran as fast as they could to the lake's shore and hid in the thickets at the foot of the dunes. While Kostya went to look for a fisherman, Dukes and Peter waited until his return. It was nighttime before he returned with news that he had been unable to find a fisherman or a boat. Scrambling though the dunes, they were scratched by barbed wire and old trenches until they reached the lake. Lake Lubans was about 18 miles long and 10 miles across, and it marked the frontier between Russia and Latvia.

After two or three hours of pulling one leg clear of the deep mud, they came upon a castaway fishing boat stranded in the rushes. With the onset of nightfall, and minus oars, they cut boughs from a tree and they slowly set off across the lake with one man bailing. All through the night they made slow progress until they came in sight of the Latvian shore. Away to the north, the artillery was booming but nothing happened on the lake. On 7 September, as they approached the beach, half a dozen Latvian guards with bayonets on the end of their rifles told them to go back. Ignoring this display, Dukes and his companions landed just in time, as the fishing boat was on the point of sinking. Rounding them up, the guards took them to a small hamlet with a guard house, where they met one of the most obnoxious commandants – worse that the German commander at Terrioki. He was a White Russian officer and he threatened to hang or shoot the trio as they were dressed in Red Russian uniforms. He was a small man with a scowling face, who smelt of liquor, and did not let up on his promise to execute them.

Dukes stated that he was English, but that did not pacify the small man. They were searched and the salt bags were tipped onto the floor. The small packets were grabbed but before they were opened, Dukes said that they were bound for the British Commissioner in Riga and he emphasised that they were for the eyes of the Commissioner only. The White Russian paused and did not open the packets. Quietening down, the commander ordered a bottle of vodka for each of them. Two days later they were delivered to the British Mission at Riga by the soldiers who guarded them. Here the British Mission relayed the intelligence via Sweden to London. Dukes managed supply a bottle of whisky to the guards who were sent back to Lake Lubans.

Kostya had tried to return to Russia but was shot and killed on the frontier. Peter Petrovich continued to work for Britain's Secret Service in Helsingfors. In the Second World War he acted as a courier for Paul Dukes and eventually retired to Sweden under the name Peter Sahlin, where he died in his eighties. He was often attacked by the communists, but survived.

Paul Dukes travelled to Reval (later Tallinn) where he was interviewed by the Provisional Government. The newspapers in Finland and Sweden quoted the story. He sailed to England and was immediately interviewed in London by the Foreign Office, the Admiralty, the War Office and the Secret Service, and retold his escape from Soviet Russia. As a civilian, he was refused a Victoria Cross and instead received a knighthood from King George V, but this was not the only award to be handed out to Paul Dukes. From Mansfield Cumming, he received a considerable amount of money wrapped in a large envelope, and a thank you for his work in Bolshevik Russia.

One day, as Dukes was leaving Mansfield Cumming's office, he met a young naval officer named Augustus Agar. For a moment neither spoke until they introduced themselves, and to their surprise, they were known to each other, having met very briefly when Gefter and Dukes sank their fishing boat as they were about to be picked up by Agar. After a debriefing in Cumming's office, they parted company. They met several times over the years and exchanged adventures and narrow escapes. Despite being in London, both men yearned to return to the frontline in Poland and Latvia. The following year Agar returned to Biorko Sound and Admiral Cowan as an Intelligence Officer, while Dukes travelled to Poland for six months without having any effect of his agents.

Their chief was Mansfield Cumming who was well into his role as leader of MI6 but he died suddenly at his home on 14 June 1923 shortly before he was due to retire.

# Chapter Sixteen

# Agar's Return to the Baltic

Gus Agar was instructed to go to Scotland to receive his Victoria Cross from the King at Balmoral. He stayed with friends at Blairgowrie, who had just moved into Butterstone House, once the home of Prime Minister William Gladstone. His stay was brief and he was called back to Buckingham Palace by the Admiralty. A railway strike had broken out and there was an emergency service to get Agar back to London.

Dressed in an ordinary reefer coat with a borrowed new sword and belt from Gieves of Bond Street, he attended his Victoria Cross investiture at 10.30 am on 9 October 1919. He spent half an hour with the king explaining his attack on the *Oleg* and the Kronstadt Raid. The king also gave him the Distinguished Service Order for his part in the Kronstadt Raid and he was asked if he would serve on the Royal Yacht, *Victoria and Albert,* which he did in January 1924. The time seemed to flash by and the king said he had a Privy Council meeting at 11.00 am. He then checked the Victoria Cross and presented it, as well as the Distinguished Service Order to Agar. On 10 October, 'C' and some of his staff, who he referred to as his 'top-mates', gave a small dinner party at the Savoy Hotel, which Agar attended. The next day, Agar caught a small coasting vessel which called into Copenhagen. He presented himself to Admiral Cowan at Biorko Sound, who elevated Agar to his Intelligence Officer. His other companions were Lieutenant Webster (his interpreter) and Claude Grahame-Watson (Flag Lieutenant), all under the guidance of Commander Chichester-Clark.

Admiral Cowan promised General Sir Hubert Gough naval support when the North West Corps got under way with the target of occupying Petrograd. The idea was to help the inshore operations on the Estonian coast using three cruisers, HMS *Dauntless, Danae* and his own ship, *Delhi.* He retained half his cruisers at Biorko Sound after the Kronstadt Raid and the rest supported the Estonian army on the right flank. Unfortunately, the White Russian front ran from the towns of Pskov to Narva and they were dismissive of the Estonians, who were despised as they were deemed an inferior ethnicity. The Estonians only wanted to push the Bolsheviks as far as their frontier, but the Whites wanted to move on to Petrograd. The armies that were pushed into the new republics of Estonia, Latvia and Lithuania found themselves fighting not just the Germans – who wanted the new colonies of Balticum – but the White Russians and the Bolsheviks – who the Germans hated. The Latvian *Landeswehr*, or volunteer soldiers, were sent to prevent the German Iron Division under the command of Major General Rudiger von der Goltz from taking over the three newly-formed republics. In February 1919 Sir Stephen Tallents was appointed British Commissioner for the Baltic Provinces during Britain's intervention in the region. He helped draw up a treaty that saw an established independence for Estonia, Latvia and Lithuania. In his report he wrote:

> In Lithuania and Latvia I found German troops in complete occupation, and these cannot be withdrawn without effective substitution unless both countries are to be resigned to the Bolsheviks. Estonia is free of Germans and shows a much stronger national spirit, but she is more hardly pressed by the Bolsheviks. The presence of many Russian refugees, coupled with the nearness of Kronstadt and Petrograd leads the Bolsheviks to regards an independent government in Estonia as a special menace. The military activity of the Germans in Latvia and Lithuania tends to strengthen the Bolshevik threat to Estonia, as it prevents the Red Armies from advancing towards East Prussia.

Incidentally, the Armistice had been signed on 11 November 1918 in the west but still, the Germans continued to fight on the eastern flank. Between May and June 1919, von der Goltz failed in his attempts to establish his Iron Division in the coastal towns of Latvia and Lithuania because of the naval presence of the British Navy. It suited the British to use the Germans as a stopgap until they sent out a strong military mission under General Gough, which took a great load off Cowan's shoulders.

A mixed force of Germans and Russians persuaded General Nikolai Yudenich to put the self-styled leader, Colonel Bermondt-Avalof, in charge of the Forces in Courland, part of Latvia. Gough insisted that the new army should be separated and the Russians should be sent to Narva. Encouraged by von der Goltz, Bermondt was promised support from his Iron Division. The mixture of German and Russian troops prompted von der Goltz to say that his Iron Division was acting on its own. Cowan, with the consent of Gough, gave Bermondt an ultimatum to leave Riga within 48 hours. Bermondt naturally ignored the warning and commenced attacking the Latvians on 6 October. By 8 October he had taken a strong position on the south bank of the River Dangava, which runs through the city.

Cowan sent two of his cruisers, *Dragon* and *Cleopatra* with two destroyers, *Abdiel* and *Vanoc*. Cowan appointed French Commodore Jean-Joseph Brisson in charge of operations. His flag was flown on the French destroyer, *L'Aisne*, the only French ship in the fleet. Bombardment forced Bermondt to withdraw from Riga and the Latvian *Landwehr* chased them out of Latvia. Bermondt's troops split up into small groups and began to loot and murder their way to East Prussia, harried all the way by the Letts. Von der Goltz gave up his idea of taking control of Latvia and Estonia, and with the remnants of the Iron Division, he evacuated to Germany by sea.

Gus Agar was present on the bridge of the *L'Aisne* and saw Bermondt's retreat. By 24 November the three Baltic States were at last free of the war factions that had dominated their lands for over a year. Agar visited the coastal towns in the destroyers *Vanoc* and *Wanderer* and saw the effects of the low economic state. He saw the wealthy families bartering their precious possessions such as furs, amber necklaces (the richest sources of amber in northern Europe), and gold and silver ornaments for cigarettes, soap, clothes and tins of biscuits. Agar even saw a woman offer her wedding ring in return for a sailor's flannel shirt to make garments for her baby.

Some of the Royal Navy sailors were forbidden to trade, but many did and sent home necklaces of amber and fur coats. Iron Crosses were exchanged for soap and the stokers on the *Dragon* traded 500 cigarettes (£1) for a baby grand piano. Days on end were spent on patrol or clearing channels through the minefields. One casualty was HMS *Vittoria*, a converted minelayer, which was torpedoed by the Bolshevik submarine *Pantera* off the island of Seiskari on 31 August 1919.

General Nikolai Yudenich was quite lackadaisical about occupying Petrograd. He eventually passed over the mission to General Rodzianko, a dashing cavalryman who knew nothing about artillery or infantry. By 3 November, all thoughts of advancing against Petrograd were abandoned. He had gone ahead and reached the outskirts of Petrograd at Tsarske Selo, where he came up against the Bolsheviks and was forced to retreat. An outbreak of typhus broke out at Narva and decimated the White Russians. Out of the original 25,000 men, only 5,000 remained. Narva became a large typhus-stricken camp where hundreds of men died, including a British officer, who wrote these dying words:

> Our aim is to save from what was once an Army a few whole bodies and sane souls ... Hospitals such as we know them do not exist ... Dead, sick, wounded, lie together on dirty straw pallets in cow sheds where no doors or windows exist, with one doctor and one sister to look after a thousand scraps of humanity ... of the remaining combatant troops there exist between four and five thousand, with Bolsheviks in front and Estonians – to them a subject race – on either side. Behind are Estonian control posts through which they have to pass linked by barbed wire. They cannot move forward nor can they as armed men, move back. They have to choose either to give up their arms and file through barbed wire into Estonian territory or seek clemency at the hands of the Bolsheviks. Once on Estonian ground they are herded into villages where typhus exists and into rooms unfit for the lowest of human beings.

In the first week of December, an armistice was called between the Estonians and the Bolsheviks. About 1,000 officers were left behind in Estonia to plead their cause with the few British Staff Officers who remained from the Military Mission. It was now December 1919 and Junior Lieutenant Augustus Agar was asked if he could intercede in the negotiations for the release of the naval prisoners. Cowan agreed and Agar donned his civilian dress and travelled to Helsingfors. Here he received two letters of introduction; one was to be given to an Estonian in Revel and the second to a colonel as part of the Professor Piip's delegation on the border at Dorpat. Agar travelled to Latvia and boarded a train at Revel. So began an extremely uncomfortable journey in a freezing carriage where they travelled at 6mph and for hours they crept along with endless stops while the engine loaded piles of wood left at the trackside. To relieve the boredom, people jumped on the train, even on the tops of the carriages, until they reached their destination. Fortunately for Agar, he had taken an overcoat with him, which was fur-lined and went some way to keep him warm. The train took one day and one night to reach their destination where he met an Estonian colonel who spoke excellent English. The colonel took him to a *dacha* where he was shown to the top floor and told to stay there as the Estonian President was in the floor below. Agar later wrote,

> I was taken to Professor Piip who was extremely courteous and kind. He apologised for my loneliness, but said it was best for my presence not to be known to anyone, otherwise the Bolsheviks might get suspicious. He had promised the Bolshevik Commissars that there would be no White Russians on their delegation, but had warned them that a British officer was coming from the Fleet who would be willing to talk to them unofficially if they wished, and was still awaiting a reply.

It was several hours before he was called to appear before the Bolshevik delegation, who were staying in another house. After days of delay, the Commissars eventually decided to meet Agar. The days passed slowly. It was something of a surprise to meet the journalist/writer Arthur Ransome, who invited Agar to visit him that evening. They spent the evening playing chess, chatting about boats and sailing and got to the subject of Russia and the lives of the peasants. After a good meal, Agar left Ransome and returned to his lonely wait until the Bolsheviks showed up.

After a few days, Professor Yoffe, the Chief Delegate and the Russian Ambassador to Germany and Japan, was assisted by Commissars Krilenko and Kreichler. Yoffe sat at a table with a Morse code device, which they used to communicate with Moscow and received messages which they relayed to the Estonians. Agar was granted two sessions of a couple of hours and let Colonel Piip do the negotiations. Krilenko was the most obnoxious of the trio and lambasted Agar for the sinking of the two battleships at Kronstadt, of which he was innocent. The two Commissars mentioned Paul Dukes but Agar denied all knowledge of the agent. Finally, Yoffe asked the intentions of the British Fleet. How long were they staying in the Gulf and what were Admiral Cowan's plans? Cowan had advised Agar to relay a message to say that the fleet was withdrawing to Copenhagen and had every intention of returning in spring. Agar stated that they had cleared mines so that food could be brought to the starving people of Estonia and Latvia. They had also lost a number of ships to mines and emphasised that food would be brought into the Gulf of Finland to prevent famine.

The atmosphere became most cordial and Agar's contribution to the talks ended. One more question was raised by Agar; when would the British naval personnel be released? Yoffe promised that they would raise this with Moscow. The captured naval personnel were sent to a converted prison outside Moscow, where they mixed with other captives who had been captured. He was asked if the prisoners were 'conscripts' or 'volunteers', to which Agar replied that they were all naval men and regarded as 'conscripts'. There were some political prisoners who were arrested by the Cheka and whose fate rested with the Commissars.

Colonel Piip was jubilant when Russia agreed to the Estonian's Independence, and Gus Agar departed for Biorko Sound, hopeful that the naval prisoners would be repatriated. Agar later wrote,

> I made the return journey to Revel in a different style. This time I was accompanied by my Estonian colonel friend in a reserved carriage with two guards posted to keep out intruders and in a quarter of the time. The Admiral was pleased to see me when I reached the flagship and to hear how the talks had gone, especially the news about our CMB prisoners and told me he was more than ever determined to stay in Biorko until the ice froze hard.

During the evacuation of Biorko Sound, the weather progressively got worse. The storms and blizzards made excavation extremely hazardous and in fact the exchange of prisoners dragged on for months. The negotiations between O'Grady (a Foreign Service civil servant) and Max Litvinov went from 1919 until April 1920. One of the nine prisoners was Lieutenant Osman Giddy; he wrote:

> During the three-day journey from Petrograd to Moscow we were given no food, except one station where soldiers brought us bread and weak tea. We were desperate with hunger and at one stop where a farm cart drew up with potatoes and carrots, we grabbed handfuls and ate them raw much to our subsequent discomfort.

Eventually we arrived at Moscow where the whole train–load of prisoners were divided into two parties. The first went to the Cheka prison; the other, of which we formed part, were consigned to the Androniev Monastery on the outskirts of the city. We refused to march, as Bremner was incapable of walking, and after much heated discussion, a cart was found for him. Our party consisted mostly Russians with as many women as men. We marched in a column. Next to us, an old lady in a faded black satin dress hobbled along on high-heeled shoes, bent under a weight of a sack bulging with old belongings. When we relieved her of this she thanked us in fluent English. She was a born a princess.

Near us, too, marched a huge man in an old fashioned frock coat, topped incongruously by a checked cap. He hailed us in an American English and was very friendly, but the princess told us to be careful as he was an agent provocateur among the prisoners ... The monastery lies on the top of a small hill overlooking the city and is most impressive. We passed through the great gateway and halted inside the walls which enclosed a cemetery and were kept there for some time, until Napier, myself and six ratings were taken to a separate building containing two large rooms. In the darkness it was some seconds before I realised the rooms were full of people. They were British soldiers ...

They were a mixed collection. Several officers captured in a White Russian mutiny at Onega, RFC officers force landed in Odessa and Murmansk, soldiers serving in regiments in North Russia ... We spent five months at this monastery. There was a large contingent of French, mainly businessmen, some Germans, a few Hungarians and Central Europeans. Conditions were appalling ... our personal cleanliness sadly deteriorated and it never left us until we left Russia. We washed under a pump in the yard until it froze ...

With the coming of the New Year the temperatures fell below zero and it was excruciating cold. We slept on trestle beds made of straw and had one small stove only, which burned wood. The soldier's ears were frostbitten as they had no woollen headgear. There was a doctor in the monastery but he had no drugs. Once the temperature dropped to 30 degrees below zero ... Such were the conditions in the new Russia. It was little better outside where the soldiers could walk freely in the city if they wished while officers were restricted to the monastery walls on the principle that privileges were for the men only and not for officers.

The British Relief Mission headed by Lieutenant Colonel Stephen Tallents, later to be Sir Stephen Tallents, wrote in his reports that,

In Lithuania and Latvia I found the German troops in complete control occupation, and those cannot be withdrawn without effective substitution unless both countries are to be resigned to the Bolsheviks. Estonia is free of the Germans and shows a much stronger national spirit, but she is more hardly pressed by the Bolsheviks. The presence of many Russian refugees, coupled with the nearness of Kronstadt and Petrograd, believed by the Bolsheviks to regard the independent government of Estonia as a special menace.

The three countries themselves desire to join forces for defence against the Bolsheviks but they are hampered by mutual jealousies. The Lithuanians resent Polish claims to the Vilna district; and the Letts are jealous of the greater activity and independence of Estonia. All three countries feel themselves to be utterly dependent on Allied support.

As Cowan's flagship the *Caledon* departed for England, the cruiser *Curacao* arrived and on 7 May he transferred his flag to her. On the 9 May, he went to Helsingfors where he congratulated Mannerheim on his country's declaration of independence. Sadly for Mannerheim, he was ousted from power within a few weeks. Cowan left for a quick visit to Libau on the Latvian coast to meet Commodore Alexander Duff, who had not yet arrived. On the morning of 13 May, 70 miles east of Revel, *Curacoa* struck a mine. Cowan was in the bath, naked. Hurridly, he donned an overcoat, and hurried to the bridge. He found that the damage had occurred to the right aft where several compartments had been flooded but there was no chance of the ship sinking. A rating was killed and several officers injured. Limping into Revel, he again transferred his flag to *Cleopatra*, while temporary repairs were made to *Curocoa*. On the 24 May, the *Galatea* arrived in Riga carrying Lieutenant-General Sir Hubert Gough, the Chief of the Allied Military Mission to the Baltic. He caused the Finns and the Germans to back off from their plans to march on Petrograd. The émigré Russian groups in London suggested that Gough was in the pay of the Bolsheviks and that he should submit to the Russians. He lasted until 25 October 1919 and was not offered further military employment.

In these circumstances it must be counted one of Tallents' and Gough's greatest achievements that they were able to impose a comprehensive armistice on 3 July. The Estonian advance, designed to prevent further German-Balt aggression, wasted in the outskirts of Riga and their troops obliged to withdraw. In his place, Tallents appointed a young Irish Guardsman from the British Mission, Lieutenant-Colonel the Hon. H.R. Alexander (Field-Marshal Lord Alexander of Tunis) as he was the only British Army officer to fight in the Baltic States. Tallents removed the German Commandant from his position in Riga and appointed himself temporary Civil Governor until a suitable Latvian could take control.

On 2 June Cowan sailed on the destroyer *Vivacious* accompanied by the *Voyager* to keep an eye out for any Bolshevik incursions. He spotted two destroyers, the *Azard* and *Gavriil* and engaged them across the minefield. Soon after the destroyers ceased fire, the submarine *L55* attempted a torpedo attack but made a hash of surfacing and was hit in the pressure hull by the *Gavriil*. *L55* sank with the loss of all hands and it was some years later she was salvaged by the Soviet Navy and used by them.

# Chapter Seventeen

# Paul Dukes as a Private Eye

Paul Dukes, having been rewarded with a large amount of money, began his travels among the mystics in the Middle East. He was a skilled author and wrote several books about spying and later about yoga. He was obviously taken with the experience of having kept a pace ahead of the Bolsheviks, including being a member of the Cheka and the Russian Communist Party. In May 1920, when Foreign Office official Reginald 'Rex' Leeper worked for the Political Intelligence Department, he was going to Poland for 'a fact-finding mission'. Paul Dukes was to accompany him on behalf of the Secret Service as his secretary and work only for expenses. Leeper was forced to withdraw from the mission and Dukes took over. He attempted to form a spy network but it came to nothing.

In the summer of 1920 the Russians and the Poles fought a battle that ranks with Waterloo for its importance in history. By 1920 the Soviet state was in turmoil following the brutal civil war. It wanted to reach Germany to spread the communist ethos to all countries in Europe, but Poland stood in the way. Russia was forced to withdraw in September, and Dukes witnessed the retaking of the fortress of Grodno by the Poles.

As I watched the shells falling over the trenches on the outskirts of the town I thought of the wrenches lying in them, hating the war, hating their leaders, and merely waiting until nightfall to creep out of the city. Though it was said that Grodno was defended by some of the best Red regiments, the retreat was precipitate. But by day or two later near Lida, they unexpectedly turned and gave battle ... One Polish division was suddenly attacked by five Red divisions. Four of the latter were beaten, but the last, the 21st, continued to fight with savage fury. Three times they bore down in massed formation. It came to a hand-to-hand fight in which the Poles were hard pressed. After the third attack, which fortunately for the Poles was weaker, an entirely unforeseen and incomprehensible event occurred. The soldiers of the 21st Soviet division killed everyone of their commissars and Communists and came over to the Poles in a body with their guns!

Sir Robert Nathan, Head of the MI6's Political Intelligence Department, described Dukes reports as 'very interesting' about the anti-Bolshevik side of the Russian Civil War. The Poles managed to keep the Russians away from their border and Lenin failed in his conquest of Europe. Dukes returned to England in November 1920, nursing ambitions to return to Russia as an agent but he never went back.

In 1921 he wrote for *The Times* about Eastern Europe, having an 'expert's eye' on what was going on. He also appeared on stage in a ballet act under the name 'Paul Dukaine'. In the early twenties, Dukes travelled to the United States where he joined a tantric yoga practice in Nyack, 15 miles from New York City. While he was in America, he met and fell in love with Margaret Rutherford Mills, stepdaughter of Walter Kissam Vanderbilt. They married on 7 November 1922 in Nyack, New York. She had been married six times to four different men. After their marriage, the couple lived at 180 Riverside Drive in New York City until Dukes divorced her in January 1929.

Dukes lectured, travelled widely, and wrote a number of books on a variety of topics, including yoga. From 1930 to 1937 he was appointed chairman of the British Continental Press, which was distributed to over 50,000 readers all over Central Europe. Just before the outbreak of the Second World War he was asked by some friends to visit Germany in order to trace the whereabouts of a wealthy Czech businessman who was in hiding in German Sudetenland, part of Czechoslovakia. He wrote about this in his book, *An Epic of the Gestapo* (1940). As a semi-private detective, his investigation solved one particular problem which rather petered out at the end. As the war clouds loomed, he moved between Prague, Mies, Berlin and Dortmund, in which he called at the Gestapo offices scattered across Czechoslovakia and Germany. He decided to undertake the invitation of a group of London businessmen to trace the whereabouts of Alfred Obry, a wealthy industrialist from Brno. Some weeks later, Obry was found on a railway bridge at Mies, badly mauled and with one hand missing. Having found the remains of Obry and unable to discover any more about the man, he left Sudetenland just as Neville Chamberlain announced that Britain was at war with Germany. In his book, Dukes wrote about the German-Soviet Pact, comparing the similarities of the two sides.

> Besides the Gestapo, the exact replica of the Cheka-Ogpu, the Press and the propaganda apparatus of both regimes is identical in character; Goebbels indeed might have been a faithful Jewish founder of the Comintern, Zinoviev-Apfelbaum. Those acquainted with the style of oratory and the argumentation of both Goebbels and Zinoviev cannot be struck by their marked resemblance, even in terminology, illustration and for inventing the cheap jibes. True, in 1936 Stalin shot his erstwhile friend Zinoviev, together with many other associates of long standing who refuse to toe the zigzag Stalin line. But Hitler likewise has liquidated no small number of his closest friends who ventured to oppose him in word or deed and no knowing what might befall Goebbels if he fails to shuffle his feet fast enough for Hitler.

During the war, he lectured on behalf of the Ministry of Information and was a director of a company that manufactured components for the British Ministry of Aircraft Production. At the end of the Second World War, the Indian Army used him to teach their soldiers the art of yoga. By the late 1940s he had appeared on television, demonstrating yoga with two female assistants when television was still in its infancy. The Coronation in 1953 saw a boom in television sets and this started the surge in the purchasing of televisions. Dukes developed a strong interest in yoga and was the author of *Yoga for the Western World* (1955) and *The Yoga of Health, Youth and Joy* (1960). He also made a series of broadcasts for the BBC on television about the subject.

In 1951 – following in the footsteps of Napoleon Bonaparte in Cairo in 1799 – Dukes spent the night alone in the King's Chamber in the heart of the Great Pyramid of Giza. What Dukes achieved was never revealed but like Bonaparte, he experienced a feeling of something supernatural. Later on he had an accident when he bade farewell to his guests and somehow managed to slip and fall under their car. Although he was in deep shock and never fully recovered, he went with his wife to Cape Town, South Africa, and died there aged 78.

# Chapter Eighteen

# Agar's Final Years

Following his Baltic experiences, Gus Agar returned to Osea Island and the Coastal Motor Boats. On 20 July 1920 he married Mary Petre, 19th Baroness Furnivall, at Westminster Cathedral. After the ceremony, a number of bluejackets harnessed themselves to the newlyweds' car and carried them in triumph to Eaton Place. Among the wedding guests were Earl Beatty and Lady Beatty, Sir Mansfield and Lady Cumming and Lieutenant Gordon Steele VC, RN. Lieutenant Commander Agar was sent to New Zealand as executive officer on HMS *Chatham*, a light cruiser assigned to the New Zealand Naval Forces, later known as the New Zealand Division, then part of the Royal Navy. In 1922, he was given command of HMS *Philomel*, an obsolete cruiser used as a training ship for the New Zealand Division. These were happy years for Agar in a friendly country with interesting work and regular cruises through the Southern Seas. In January 1924, he was reappointed captain of the Royal Yacht *Victoria and Albert*, another pleasant duty which lasted until January 1925.

Admiral Sir Roger Keyes asked for Agar in April 1926 and he was given command of HMS *Witch*, leader of the 4th Destroyer Flotilla, assigned to the Mediterranean Fleet. The flotilla consisted of four ships which were disbanded in 1936. As Agar and his wife were living apart, it had an adverse effect on his chances of promotion which kept him from reaching the position of flag rank. He spent the next few years on shore, including a position of naval advisor to the New Zealand Delegation at the London Naval Conference in 1930. On 30 September 1930, he was placed in command of the sloop, HMS *Scarborough*, attached to the North America and West Indies Squadron. He served on the ship until September 1932, during which time he married Ina Hirst in Bermuda in February 1932. In March 1933, he was involved in a seaplane accident. It crashed during a squall on the Acushnet River on a visit to New Bedford, Massachusetts. Both the pilot and the other passenger were killed, while Gus suffered injuries from which he recovered. When he was well enough, he attended a Senior Officer's Course at Greenwich and was promoted to captain.

In early 1936 he commanded anti-aircraft cruiser *Curlew*, part of the Reserve Fleet at the Nore. In 1937 he was given command of light cruiser HMS *Emerald*, his favourite ship and which was the fastest vessel at 35 knots in the Royal Navy. The *Emerald* was attached to the East India Station for July 1937 to July 1938, but after serving as captain of the Royal Navy College at Greenwich, he returned to the *Emerald* in the summer of 1939.

When Britain declared war on Germany on 3 September 1939, he was ordered onto the Northern Patrol between the Faroe Islands and Iceland to block any German Merchant ships trying to return to their homeland. Another duty was to intercept neutral ships heading to Germany and confiscate contraband. In October 1939, he received a 'Top Secret' order to sail to Plymouth where he was ordered to cross the Atlantic. The order read:

> Two million pound in gold bars is to be embarked in each ship to Halifax. A railway truck is expected to be placed alongside each ship about 01.00 am, 7 October. Each truck is expected to contain 148 boxes each weighing 130 lbs. The total number of boxes is numbered Z298 to Z741 inclusive. Guards are to be put on each truck on arrival at the ship ... Adequate steps are to be taken for supervision of each box from unloading from truck to stowage in ship. Finally a receipt is to be forwarded to C-in-C Western Approaches on attached form.

On 7 October 1939, in an operation named 'Operation Fish', *Emerald* sailed from Plymouth to Halifax, Nova Scotia carrying £58 million in gold bullion from the Bank of England to safe storage in Canada until the threat of German invasion had passed. The crew were fitted out in tropical whites to confuse the German agents, who expected the cruiser to head south to the hotter climate. They were accompanied by two old battleships, HMS *Revenge* and *Resolution*, the old cruiser *Caradoc* and *Emerald*'s sister ship, *Enterprise*. They were ordered to pay for war materials before the later introduction of the American Lend Lease. The gold was transferred to the Canadian National Railway and kept under wraps in Montreal. In November, they conveyed another cargo of gold bullion to Halifax. In February 1940 *Emerald* ran into some of the heaviest seas Agar had ever encountered. Convening the UK's gold reserves, they reached Halifax with the *Emerald* losing her ship's boats, rafts, depth charges and even had the misfortune to lose her spotter aeroplane, a Fairey *Kingdom*. In a semi-wrecked state, she returned to Southampton on 15 February 1940 for repairs. By the spring of 1940, *Emerald* carried a further £10 million gold bullion to Canada, accompanied by the destroyers HMS *Cossack* and *Atherstone*.

On 18 October the *Emerald* accompanied a large convoy made up of American munitions for the war effort. Since the *Emerald* had been designed for more tropical climates, the ship was very uncomfortable and the Canadian Red Cross provided warm gear to face the winter storms. As they crossed the Atlantic, they lost two merchant ships to U-boats. The Canadian troops were on the larger merchant ships and *Emerald* continued to keep a watch on the larger vessels. The convoy duties of *Emerald* during the terrible winter of 1939–40 were appalling and finally, Agar's tour of duty was completed in June 1940 after escorting a contingent of Canadian troops on the *Empress of Australia* to Iceland. He was assigned to command the destroyer leader HMS *Malcolm*, as head of the 16th Destroyer Flotilla based in Harwich. Agar was in charge of 'Operation Lucid' in September 1940 in an attempt to destroy the wooden invasion barges at Boulogne and Calais. He was accompanied by four ancient oil tankers filled with incendiary fuel know as 'Agar's Special Mixture'. The tankers were in poor condition and unfit for such mission with bad weather and mechanical breakdowns, which forced several cancellations. The final attempt was when Agar was on board destroyer *Hambledown* when it hit an acoustic mine mid-Channel and was severely damaged. She was towed away from the French coast after being shelled by German shells without being hit. By now it was too late to destroy the invasion barges as they were sent to the main rivers and used to convey goods throughout Germany and France.

On 25 November 1940, Agar was appointed Chief Staff Officer to the Rear Admiral Commanding Coastal Forces. This was a crucial time as the Germans were vigorously attacking coastal convoys from east Scotland and north-east England to London. The toll of the East Coast convoys was in danger of the E-boats making a quick dash from the ports in the Low Countries. British Rail was unable to carry the coal and other materials and had to rely on the Royal Navy to defend the convoys.

Besides Gus Agar's efforts to keep the E-boats away from the east coast convoys, it was Lieutenant Commander Richard Hichens who broke up the E-boats attacks. He was awarded the DSO and Bar and the DSC and two Bars but no Victoria Cross. Between November 1940 and July 1941, Agar had to work hard to keep the E-boats away from the merchant convoys but relied on the speed of Hichens Motor Gun Boats to subdue to German high-speed boats.

On August 1941 Agar was appointed captain of the heavy cruiser HMS *Dorsetshire*. The ship carried a catapult-operated reconnaissance aircraft, the Supermarine Walrus, which had a great range and was designed to find and destroy enemy commerce raiders. She was assigned convoy protection duty from Scotland to South Africa, with a stop en route at Freetown, Sierra Leone. Based at Freetown, *Dorsetshire* worked with HMS *Newcastle* and later HMS *Dunedin* and *Devonshire*. For a while they were joined by aircraft carrier HMS *Eagle* and their remit was to protect Allied shipping in the South Atlantic from German commerce raiders. In particular, the main targets were the supply ships which transferred fresh supplies and oil to the submarines and surface raiders. Without the support of the supply ships, the submarines would have to withdraw. One surface raider was the *Atlantis*, which had sunk 145,000 tonnage between 1939 and 1941. The *Devonshire* caught up with *Atlantis*, and after an exchange of fire, the surface raider disappeared beneath the waves. A week later, on 1 December, the *Dorsetshire* came upon German supply ship *Python*. Agar fired two torpedoes, one at the front and one behind in a warning effort to surrender. Unable to escape, *Python* scuttled herself and Agar left the German crew to wait for a submarine. One of the U-boats heading for the *Python* spotted HMS *Dunedin* and sank her, leaving only 4 officers and 63 men out of 486 who survived the sinking.

Agar berthed his ship at the naval base at Simon's Town on 7 December. She was immediately assigned to escort a convoy of troops just arriving from Halifax. The *Dorsetshire* guided the Canadians to Bombay but quickly returned to Durban to escort another convoy to Aden and Bombay. Their objective was to bypass the island of Madagascar held by the Vichy French, but they were not attacked. *Dorsetshire* was given the task of extracting the civilians from Singapore before the Japanese overran the island, and getting them to safety to Colombo, Ceylon. In between time, Agar was to transport and land a party of 100 Royal Marines on the coast of Burma to harass the invading Japanese forces and to take off the last remnants before Rangoon fell on 8 March 1942. The *Dorsetshire* returned to Colombo to refit her engine and install anti-aircraft guns, while the Commander-in-Chief, Admiral James Somerville, had moved the main part of his fleet further west to the Maldives. He ordered Agar to go to Colombo to complete his refit which involved cleaning the boilers and dismantling his machinery. Sadly there was little time and *Dorsetshire* was put to sea incomplete. Agar received word that the Japanese navy had entered the Bay of Bengal. The *Dorsetshire* was part of the scratch fleet of obsolete battleships with two small aircraft carriers and some attached cruisers hurriedly put together to halt the Japanese naval advance into the Indian Ocean. Somerville's objective was to keep the sea lanes open to India via the Persian Gulf and the Eighth Army in Egypt.

On 4 April 1942 an urgent message alerted Agar to go to the Operations Room at Colombo. A Catalina flying boat had just reported that it was shadowing a large force of Admiral Chiuchi Nagumo's fleet, consisting of enemy carriers, accompanied by battleships, steering west from the Malacca Straits directly to Ceylon. His fleet of five carriers inflicted severe losses on Somerville's fleet, including a light aircraft carrier, two destroyers, one convette, five other vessels and cruisers *Dorsetshire* and *Cornwall*. Somerville ordered Agar's cruisers to leave Colombo and join him at the Maldives. It took six hours to reassemble their ship's machinery and get her ready for the Maldives. Agar and his fellow cruiser, *Cornwall*, left Colombo at high speed at 10.00 pm on 4 April. They had no idea of any Japanese dive bombers in the area and headed for the Maldives. The rendezvous point was too far to the east and a more westerly point would have saved the two cruisers. As *Cornwall* had been built in the 1920s, she only managed 28 knots. The following day, the two cruisers were sighted by a spotter plane from the Japanese carrier *Tone* about 200 miles south-west of Ceylon. The dive bombers began their attack of the port of Colombo and destroyed the radio tower, losing contact with the two cruisers.

At daybreak on Easter Sunday, Agar received a signal that the Japanese Fleet was only 120 miles south of Colombo. At 11.30 am a patrol plane spotted the cruisers and relayed the message to the carriers. A wave of Aichi D3A dive bombers had taken off from three aircraft carriers and began their attack on the two cruisers. Agar broke his radio silence to tell

Somerville of his decision to reach the rendezvous point 90 miles away. Onboard the *Dorsetshire*, Captain Agar received a message from destroyer HMS *Tenedos* that it had spotted a Japanese scout plane to the north-east. Somerville advised Agar to return to Colombo by the morning where they would not be exposed in the open ocean without cover. Instead, Agar turned his small force towards Port T (Addu Atoll) in the Maldives. He believed he could get his ships out of air range by the morning of 5 April, but instead, he found himself exposed to a mass dive bombing attack.

At 1.00 pm the dive bombers unleashed their bombs on the *Dorsetshire* and the only thing that Agar could do was prepare to retaliate. The slowest ship in the motley task force was the old monitor, HMS *Erebus*. Agar would have been flattered that the Japanese reconnaissance pilot misidentified his heavy cruiser, the armed monitor and merchant cruiser HMS *Hector* as battleships, while his destroyer was tagged as a cruiser, and HMS *Hollyhock* as a destroyer.

On 8 July 1958, the *Evening Standard*, having interviewed several seamen, reported quite accurately the following account:

On Easter Saturday 1942, as the Far East crumbled under relentless pressure from Japanese air, land and sea attacks, the cruiser *Dorsetshire* was steaming at 30 knots south-south-west from Ceylon, heading for a rendezvous in the Indian Ocean. Six hundred yards astern was her sister ship, the 10,000 ton *Cornwall*. Intelligence reports warned that a powerful Jap force was steaming at high speed for Ceylon to deliver a knock-out blow. The two British cruisers were due to rendezvous the British Fleet at 4 pm.

Captain Agar commanding *Dorsetshire*, who won the Victoria Cross in the Kronstadt fortress action in 1919, was on the bridge just before noon, when a plane was sighted astern. As the British Fleet had carriers there was nothing alarming about that – until the plane was seen to have floats. It was Japanese and Agar ordered the ships to action stations. Within seconds men were dashing to the guns, magazines and shell rooms. Suddenly the radar operators hunched over their crude sets reported large numbers of enemy aircraft approaching. Suddenly the ships were swamped with bombs. One bursting forwards brought the foremast crashing down; another further aft brought the main mast down. A third blasted the funnel. A fourth brought down the other two. Other bombs crashed through the thin steel shell of her hull to blast the engine room and start fires. The second in command, Commander C.W. Byas was riddled with splinters and fell to the deck.

Slowly the ship slowed down. Quickly she heeled to 30 degrees and Captain Agar moved to the back of the bridge to see if anything could be done to save her. Both masts were down and all three funnels were ablaze with a big fire raging amidships. There was no hope and Agar gave the order to abandon ship. Officers and ratings on the bridge clambered down blast-twisted ladders to the upper deck. Other men dragged badly wounded shipmates with them. On the fo'c'sle a group of seamen from the forward turrets were hesitating by the guard rails. 'Have we done our job, sir? Can we go now?' one of them called to Lieutenant B.C. Durant, the navigator.

Slowly *Dorsetshire* heeled over. Her sides were almost horizontal and survivors clambered along the hull and slid round the turn of the bilge into the sea. A few moments later they gathered round rafts and wreckage as the stern of the ship lifted high into the air, her screws still slowly turned for a moment, then slid quietly down to the sea bed. A minute or two later and four miles away, *Cornwall*, too sank in a cloud of smoke and steam. While more than 1,200 men struggled in the water, the Jap planes flew low over them and machine-gunned them. One of the men killed was Surgeon-Commander F.C.E. Bamford, *Dorsetshire*'s doctor. The swimmers found the badly wounded Commander Byas and lashed him to a floating door. Lieutenant Durant found a boat riddled with bullet holes and gathered some men together to start plugging the holes. Other survivors clutched at two small rafts, a floating net, the chart table and even the butcher's block which had floated clear as the ship sank.

Soon more debris floated past, including tins of lard which the men rubbed on their skins to protect themselves from the blistering sun. Fuel oil spread over the water and started the eyes smarting. But Captain Agar, one of whose lungs had been hurt when he was sucked down by the sinking ship, realised that his men's greatest danger was from sharks. He ordered the men to pull the bodies of their dead shipmates into one area. Then he set as many survivors as possible swimming round in a circle, frightening the sharks away.

Slowly the afternoon wore on. The sea was still calm with a slight swell and was quite warm. As darkness fell, the men started singing, mainly songs of the slow sentimental type. With desperate slowness, night gave way to dawn. In the two boats and on the rafts, the first job was to throw overboard the men who had died during the night. Then came the time to issue rations. The men took it in turns to form an orderly queue and one mouthful of milk from tins in the boat and a quarter of a ship's biscuit was given to each man. Occasionally sharks were seen round the perimeter of the human stockade. When the men were on the crest of a gentle swell they could see survivors from *Cornwall* swimming four miles away.

As the sun rose, the men were listless and silent. In the afternoon a second ration of milk and biscuits was issued. Then the officers swam round the rafts to talk to the men. At sunset someone in the water shouted that he thought he could see a speck on the horizon. Lieutenant Durant stood up in the boat with a pair of binoculars and relayed to the captain, 'It is definitely the foretop of a warship.' The next moment he wished he had been less positive, because the Chief Boatswain's Mate produced his pipe and piped 'The Navigating Officer says he can see a warship.' A tremendous cheer broke out.

The warship was the cruiser *Enterprise* reluctant to abandon the search, said, without much hope or reason, 'There is still some light – hold on with the present leg of the search for another ten minutes.' Seven minutes later, the startled lookout reported 'Something in the water.' Within a short time 1,122 survivors of *Dorsetshire* and *Cornwall* have been taken onboard the three ships. But 424 officers and men had been killed or died of wounds in that brief but deadly air attack.

With the dive bombers attacking the *Dorsetshire* and *Cornwall*, in eight minutes both ships were sunk. Agar was on the bridge and suffered shrapnel wounds in his leg which turned septic after being in the water for so long. When the ship sank, Agar was dragged down with her and suffered the bends coming up. On the surface he swallowed oil, which reacted with one of his lungs, and affected his fitness for further seagoing duty. He commented that the sea was covered with oil, which helped keep the sharks away. Captain Agar worked hard to save his men, picking up the wounded in a whaler, gathering up stragglers and calmly addressed the men in the sea. A total of 424 men had been killed, and 1,122 survived in the sea until rescue came thirty-two hours later. A Fairey Swordfish found them in the water and an hour later the light cruiser *Enterprise* picked up some survivors. The *Panther* arrived to rescue the rest of the survivors and the destroyer *Paladin* took onboard the ailing Gus Agar. After a short stay in Bombay, Agar was sent to a hospital in South Africa. His leg recovered but his lung gave him trouble, although this he managed to disguise. He was 52 and had completed 37 years of active duty before being sent to Belfast to supervise the building of the new aircraft carrier, HMS *Unicorn*. He still had trouble with his lung and was placed on the Retired List in 1943. Once he had gained his health back, he was appointed Commodore and served as President and Captain of the Royal Naval College at Greenwich from 1943 to 1946, when he retired.

As a civilian, he moved to Alton in Hampshire where he wrote three books about his life in the navy. He then went on to farm strawberries and wrote another book about the subject. He was also on hand to witness the transportation of his old Motor Boat, *CMB-4* from the Thames to Southampton, which was diverted through his town. There is a picture of Augustus Agar saluting the old boat as she was taken to Thornycroft's in Southampton. He died at the age of 78 on 30 December 1968 and is buried at Alton Cemetery.

Admiral Walter Cowan wrote a report of his stay in the Baltic, in which he defended the five main countries, Estonia, Latvia, Lithuania, Finland and Poland from being absorbed into the Bolshevik web. He had championed Lieutenant Augustus Agar in his sinking of the *Oleg* and the destruction of the battleships, *Andrei Pervozvanni*, *Petropavlovsk* and the submarine depot vessel, *Pamiat Azova*, renamed *Dvina*. He even appointed him to be a Naval Intelligence agent for the Navy. He sent his final report to the Admiralty, in which he wrote:

> Our role was to keep order and prevent oppression in the Baltic until stable and humane Governments are formed by all peoples on its shores. You will agree with me that our service out here was hard

and disagreeable when so many have well earned rest and happiness; yet out of the Navy has scarcely ever had a worthier aim or, if it succeeds, one which will bring it more honour and affection in the world, particularly out here among peoples who have been kept from oppression and saved from starvation. So I ask you to help me see it through with the same splendid staunchness that I have had from you all through my nine months service here; and I hope that what I have said will remove the perplexity which must be in many of your minds. In one word, we are the police of a very disturbed district, and our great hope is to end as the saviours of thousands of lives by winning our way through the minefields with food for Petrograd.

By the end of the Second World War, the Baltic States were soon absorbed into the USSR, and became part of the Iron Curtain that repelled the West. By the 1980s, the leadership of Mikhail Gorbachev had retreated Russia to its borders. East and West Germany were once again a German nation; the Czech Republic and Slovakia had parted their ways; and Ukraine had appeared as a vast country but lost the Crimean Peninsula and Russia nibbling away at its southern tip. In the Baltic, the southern nations emerged and were recognised as being independent countries. They, with the other nations, were absorbed into the West and were admitted to the United Nations, joined the European Union and NATO.

# Bibliography

*Ace of Spies* by Robert Bruce Lockhart. Pub. 1967

*Baltic Episode* by Augustus Agar. Pub. 1963

*Freeing the Baltic – 1918–1920* by Geoffrey Bennett. Pub. 1964

*Go Spy the Land* by George Alexander Hill. Pub. 2014

*Handbook for Travellers in Russia* edited by John Murray. Pub. 1868

*Memoirs of a British Agent* by R.H.Bruce-Lockhart. Pub. 2002

*MI6* by Nigel West. Pub. 1983

*One Woman's Story* by Mary Britnieva. Pub. 1934

*Operation Kronstadt* by Harry Ferguson. Pub. 2008

*Reminiscences of a Courier – Archives of the Russian Revolution* by A.Gefter. Pub.
  Slovo Publishers 1924.

*Red Dusk and the Morrow* by Paul Dukes. Pub. 1922

*Russian Roulette: A Deadly Game* by Giles Milton. Pub. 2013

*Secret Service* by Christopher Andrew. Pub. 1985

*Sound of Guns: The Story of Sir Walter Cowan* by Lionel Dawson. Pub. 1949

*The First Casualty* by Phillip Knightley. Pub. 1975

*The Journal of the Victoria Cross Society* (Oct 2005–Oct 2006). Edited by Brian
  Best

*The Life of Arthur Ransome* by Hugh Brogan. Pub. 1984

*The Lockhart Plot* by Jonathan Schneer. Pub. 2020

*The Mammoth Book of War Correspondents* edited by Jon. E. Lewis. Pub. 2001

*The Quest for 'C' –Mansfield Cumming and the founding of the Secret Service*. By
  Alan Judd. Pub. 1999

*The Russian Civil War 1918–22* by David Bullock. Pub. 2008

*The Story of 'ST25'* by Paul Dukes. Pub. 1938

*Warsaw 1920* by Adam Zamoyski. Pub. 2008.